Gourmet Appetizer
COOKBOOK

by Naomi Arbit and June Turner

Ideals Publishing Corp.
Milwaukee, Wisconsin

Contents

ISBN 0-89542-618-8 295

COPYRIGHT © MCMLXXIX BY NAOMI ARBIT AND JUNE TURNER
MILWAUKEE, WIS. 53201
ALL RIGHTS RESERVED. PRINTED AND BOUND IN U.S.A.

Cover Recipes:
Corsican Combo, p. 56
Deviled Shrimp, p. 48
Fondue of Brie, p. 5
Mushroom Turnovers, p. 36

Pictured opposite:
Sautéed Nuts, p. 41
Virginia Peanuts, p. 41

Cheeses

SAUCY CHEDDAR SPREAD

1 8-oz. pkg. sharp Cheddar cheese,
    grated
¼ c. margarine or butter
2 T. chili sauce
1 t. Worcestershire sauce
½ small onion, minced

Combine all ingredients, mixing well. Serve with crackers or rye slices. Makes about 1 cup.

POTTED CHEESE

1 lb. sharp Cheddar cheese, grated
¼ c. butter
1 T. brandy
1 T. mustard
    Dash of Tabasco sauce

Combine all ingredients, mixing well. Chill and serve with crackers. Serves 6 to 8.

SWISS CHEESE AND OLIVE SPREAD

2 c. grated Swiss cheese
3 T. chopped pimiento-stuffed olives,
    drained
2 T. chopped green pepper
    Mayonnaise to moisten

Thoroughly mix together all ingredients, making a thick paste; spread on toast rounds. Serves 12 to 16.

CUCUMBER-CHEESE SANDWICH

1 8-oz. pkg. cream cheese
1 8-oz. pkg. Roquefort or blue cheese
½ c. mayonnaise
1 t. Worcestershire sauce
    Thin bread, white or wheat,
    crusts removed
1 medium-size cucumber, thinly sliced
1 c. snipped chives
    Garlic salt (optional)

Mix together cheeses, mayonnaise, and Worcestershire sauce until smooth. Cut bread slices into quarters. Spread cheese mixture on bread, top each with a cucumber slice, a light dusting of garlic salt and a sprinkle of chives. Makes 2 to 3 dozen.

EASY FONDUE

8 oz. Muenster cheese, shredded
2 T. flour
1 c. beer
½ t. prepared mustard
¼ t. garlic powder
    Bread cubes or sausage cubes

Combine cheese and flour. Heat beer in fondue pot until bubbles rise to surface (do not boil). Add a small amount of cheese at a time, stirring constantly. Let each amount melt before adding more cheese. Continue stirring until mixture bubbles lightly. Stir in mustard and garlic. Dip cubes of bread or sausage in fondue. Makes 4 servings.

CHEESE FONDUE

1 8-oz. pkg. Muenster cheese, shredded
2 T. flour
1 c. beer
½ t. prepared mustard
   Cubes of bread or
   Frankfurters cut into 1-inch pieces

Toss cheese with flour. Heat beer in fondue pot or chafing dish until it bubbles (do not boil). Add small amounts of cheese mixture, stirring constantly; let cheese melt before adding more. Continue stirring until mixture bubbles lightly. Stir in mustard. Serve hot with bread or frankfurters for dipping. Makes 4 servings.

BLUE CHEESE MOLD

2 3-oz. pkgs. cream cheese, softened
1 4-oz. pkg. blue cheese
1 t. Worcestershire sauce
2 T. snipped parsley
½ t. salt
½ t. paprika
1 envelope unflavored gelatin
2 T. cold water
½ c. hot water
1 c. heavy cream, whipped

Mix cheeses together until well blended. Stir in Worcestershire sauce, parsley, salt, and paprika and set aside. Soften gelatin in cold water. Add hot water and stir until gelatin is dissolved. Blend in cheese mixture and chill until mixture is slightly thickened. Fold in whipped cream and pour into a lightly oiled 6-cup mold. Chill until firm. Makes 10 to 12 servings.

SWISS FONDUE

1 clove garlic, split
1 c. dry white wine
½ lb. Swiss cheese, shredded
½ lb. Gruyere cheese, shredded
   Dash of pepper, nutmeg and paprika
1 T. cornstarch
¼ c. Kirsch or cherry brandy
1 loaf French or Italian bread, cubed
   (leave crust on one side)

Rub the inside of saucepan, chafing dish, or fondue pot with garlic. Add wine and heat. Add shredded cheese in small amounts, stirring constantly with wooden spoon until smooth and melted. Add seasonings and remove from heat. Mix cornstarch and Kirsch into paste; add to fondue. Return to heat and cook another 2 minutes stirring constantly. Serve, keeping hot over burner, stirring occasionally. Spear bread cubes through soft side into crust and dip in fondue. Serves 24.

Note: It is best to make fondue in a heavy saucepan on the stove and then transfer to chafing dish or fondue pot before serving.

FONDUE OF BRIE

1½ to 2 lb. round of Brie cheese
1 c. toasted almond slices
   Melba toast or sliced hard rolls

One hour before serving, place Brie, bottom up, on a flameproof platter. After about 30 minutes, remove the thin layer of crust. Place under a preheated broiler until surface bubbles. Garnish with toasted almonds. Serve hot surrounded with toast or roll slices. Serves 18 to 24.

SHERRIED CHEESE

1 8-oz. pkg. cream cheese, softened
½ 10½-oz. can beef consommé
1 T. sherry
½ cucumber, drained and minced

Mix together all ingredients well. Chill and serve with rye chips. Serves 4 to 6.

WATERCRESS SPREAD

2 3-oz. pkgs. cream cheese with chives, softened
¼ c. butter, softened
1 T. minced onion
1 T. mayonnaise
1 bunch watercress, minced

Blend cheese with butter, onion, and mayonnaise until smooth. Blend in watercress. Spread on trimmed, thin white or whole wheat bread for sandwiches or serve with melba toast. Makes 1½ cups.

MOCK BOURSIN

1 8-oz. pkg. cream cheese
1 clove garlic, minced
1 t. caraway seed
1 t. basil
1 t. dill weed
½ t. Worcestershire sauce
Lemon pepper

Blend first 6 ingredients together. On waxed paper, pat into a flattened circle. Sprinkle another piece of waxed paper with lemon pepper; roll all sides of the cheese in the pepper. Shape again into a flattened circle. Wrap in plastic wrap and chill at least a day before serving. Serve with crackers. Serves 4 to 6.

CHEESE PUFFS

1 egg white
½ t. cream of tartar
¼ t. salt
1½ c. grated medium or sharp Cheddar cheese
18 buttered bread rounds

Beat egg white with cream of tartar and salt until light and frothy. Stir in cheese and mix well. Mound mixture on bread rounds and place on a baking sheet. Broil about 4 inches from burner for 3 to 5 minutes or until golden brown. Makes 18 puffs.

CHEESE SPREAD

8 oz. sharp Cheddar cheese, shredded
1 8-oz. pkg. cream cheese
¼ c. beer
½ t. dry mustard
    Dash of cayenne pepper
1 T. snipped green onions or chives
1 t. chopped pimiento, optional

Combine cheeses, beer, mustard, and cayenne; mix until well-blended. Stir in green onion and pimiento, if desired. Chill several hours. Serve at room temperature with crackers. Makes 1¾ cups.

CHEESE AND NUT SPREAD

¼ lb. Cheddar cheese, grated
1 3-oz. pkg. cream cheese, softened
¼ c. sour cream
¼ t. garlic powder
½ t. Worcestershire sauce
½ c. finely chopped nuts, (walnuts or pecans)

Combine all ingredients and mix thoroughly. Serve with crackers. Makes 1½ cups.

CHEESE TARTS

CRUSTADES

24 slices of thin bread, crusts trimmed
    Softened butter

Roll out bread slice to flatten slightly. Cut bread into 2½-inch rounds and butter both sides. Ease circle into miniature muffin tins so that edges ruffle. Place filling in center and bake in a 325° oven for 15 to 18 minutes until golden brown. Serve warm.

FILLINGS

24 cubes of Cheddar, Muenster, Swiss or blue cheese
24 t. of clam spread
24 t. of cream cheese, olive spread
24 t. of ham spread

Crustades may also be baked empty and filled with cold spread, such as chicken, ham, shrimp, or egg salad.

Pictured opposite:
Cheese Tarts

CHEESE BALLS

1 8-oz. pkg. Swiss cheese, grated or shredded
½ c. margarine or butter, softened
1 t. mustard
1 t. Worcestershire sauce
2 T. dry sherry
Dash of Tabasco
½ to 1 c. finely chopped walnuts

Mix all ingredients together and shape into 1-inch balls. Spear with toothpicks. Makes about 3 to 4 dozen.

QUICK CREAM CHEESE SPREAD

1 8-oz. pkg. cream cheese
Pepper Jelly
Crackers

Top cream cheese with Pepper Jelly, surround with crackers and serve. Makes about 1 cup.

PEPPER JELLY

¼ c. chopped sweet red pepper
¾ c. chopped green pepper
5½ c. sugar
1½ c. white vinegar
1 6-oz. bottle liquid pectin

In a saucepan, combine pepper, sugar, and vinegar; boil 3 minutes. Remove from heat and set aside for 5 minutes. Stir in pectin. Pour into sterilized jars and seal. Makes 4 to 5 4-oz. jars.

READY RYE APPETIZERS

1 3 to 4-oz. pkg. sliced smoked beef, snipped
1 4-oz. pkg. shredded Cheddar cheese
1 can pitted ripe olives, sliced
1 c. mayonnaise
Rye crackers

Combine first 4 ingredients, mixing well. Spread about 1 tablespoon on each rye cracker. Bake in a 375° oven for 5 to 7 minutes or until bubbly, or 45 seconds in a microwave oven. Makes about 3 dozen.

CAMEMBERT CHEESE SPREAD

1 8-oz. pkg. camembert cheese, softened
½ c. margarine or butter, softened
2 T. brandy
1 T. sour cream
¼ c. toasted sesame seed

Combine all ingredients, mixing well. Chill for 48 hours. Before serving, bring to room temperature. Serve with assorted crackers. Makes about 1 cup.

OLIVE-NUT SPREAD

1 8-oz. pkg. cream cheese, softened
1 T. mayonnaise
1 4½-oz. can ripe olives, chopped
½ t. garlic powder (optional)
¼ to ½ c. chopped nuts

Combine all ingredients, mixing thoroughly. Spread on bread rounds, chill, then serve. Makes about 1 cup.

CHEESE BALLS

1 8-oz. pkg. cream cheese
1 4-oz. pkg. blue cheese
1 T. grated onion
Finely snipped parsley *or* chopped nuts

Combine cheeses and onion. Form into small balls and roll in parsley or nuts. Serve on toothpicks. Makes about 1½ cups.

CRUNCHY SPREAD

1 8-oz. pkg. cream cheese, softened
¼ c. mayonnaise
1 medium onion, minced
1 large tomato, chopped
1 stalk celery, minced
5 to 6 slices chipped beef, torn in bits

Combine all ingredients, mixing well. Serve with crackers or toast. Makes about 1¼ cups.

CHEESE ROUNDS

½ c. mayonnaise
½ c. grated Parmesan cheese
1 T. minced onion

Combine all ingredients, mixing well. Spread on melba toast. Broil until bubbly. Makes 1½ to 2 dozen.

SAVORY CHEESE SPREAD

½ c. grated Cheddar cheese or
    cheese spread
2 T. mayonnaise
¼ t. dry mustard
1 T. chopped ripe olives
2 t. anchovy paste
1 t. lemon juice
    Salt and pepper to taste

Combine all ingredients, mixing well. Spread on whole wheat bread rounds. Serves 6 to 8.

SESAME CHEESE LOG

1 8-oz. pkg. cream cheese, softened
1 4-oz. pkg. blue cheese, softened
½ c. margarine, softened
½ c. chopped black olives
1 T. Worcestershire sauce
1 T. chopped chives
1 T. snipped parsley
½ c. toasted sesame seed

Combine all ingredients except sesame seed, mixing well. Form into a log or ball; roll in sesame seed. Serve with crackers or melba toast. Serves 8 to 10.

ALMOND OR PISTACHIO CHEESE LOG

1 c. shredded Cheddar cheese
1 16-oz. pkg. cream cheese, softened
2 t. prepared mustard
½ c. slivered almonds or chopped
    pistachio nuts

Cream cheeses with mustard. On waxed paper, shape into a roll 9 inches long. Roll in nuts, wrap in plastic and chill. Let stand at room temperature about 30 minutes before serving. Serves 12 to 16.

PARTY CHEESE SPREAD

1 c. Cheddar cheese spread
1 3-oz. pkg. cream cheese
1 c. small curd cottage cheese
¼ c. orange liqueur
½ c. chopped walnuts

Mix cheeses together until smooth. Add liqueur and nuts. Shape into ball or place in bowl; chill for several hours. Serve at room temperature with crackers. Makes 2 cups.

ANOTHER BOURSIN

1 8-oz. pkg. cream cheese, softened
¼ c. mayonnaise
1 clove garlic, minced
1 t. lemon juice
¼ t. salt
2 t. snipped chives
2 t. snipped parsley
1 t. freshly ground pepper

Mix together all ingredients except pepper. Form into a flattened circle. Sprinkle with pepper. Chill; serve with crackers. Serves 4 to 6.

Dips

GUACAMOLE

1 c. mashed avocado
1 T. lemon juice
1 t. salt
1½ t. grated onion

Note: For variety, add 1 or more of the following:

    Dash of Tabasco
1 t. curry powder
1 t. Worcestershire sauce
½ t. chili powder

Combine all ingredients and mix well. Chill several hours. Serve with chips or crackers. Makes 1 cup Guacamole.

DIPPERS

Scallions
Green beans
Carrot or celery sticks
Fresh pineapple spears
Radishes
Green pepper slices
Cucumber or zucchini rounds
Cauliflowerets
Mushrooms
Kohlrabi slices
Turnip slices
Asparagus spears

Serve an assortment of these vegetables and fruits with the usual chips, pretzel sticks, and crackers.

CORN CHIPS

½ c. cornmeal (yellow or white)
1 t. salt
¾ c. boiling water
2 T. butter
    Sesame, celery, or poppy seeds

Mix together cornmeal, salt, water, and butter. On foil-lined cookie sheets, place 1 to 2 teaspoonfuls of batter 2 inches apart. Sprinkle with choice of seeds; bake in a 425° oven about 8 minutes. Let harden slightly before removing to cool on rack. Makes 48 2-inch chips.

SHERRIED ONION DIP

½ c. sherry
½ pkg. onion soup mix
1 pt. sour cream or half and half

In a saucepan, warm sherry; add soup mix. Set aside for 30 minutes, then blend in sour cream. Serve with raw vegetables or crackers. Makes about 2½ cups dip.

CAVIAR DIP

1 c. yogurt or sour cream
1 4-oz. jar red caviar
1 t. minced parsley (optional)
1 T. grated onion

Combine all ingredients, mixing well. Serve with small rounds of melba toast for dipping. Makes about 1½ cups dip.

Pictured opposite:
Guacamole
Dippers

GREEN GODDESS DIP

1 c. cream-style cottage cheese
1 T. anchovy paste
4 sprigs of parsley
1 t. Worcestershire sauce
½ t. dry mustard
1 garlic clove
1 T. minced green onion or chives
4 T. mayonnaise

Place all ingredients in a blender or food processor and blend until smooth. Refrigerate several hours before serving with assorted bite-sized raw vegetables. Makes about 1¼ cups.

CLAM DIP

1 7½-oz. can minced clams, drained
1 T. clam juice
6 drops Tabasco sauce
½ t. Worcestershire sauce
½ t. salt
1 t. minced onion
1 8-oz. pkg. cream cheese or 1 c. cottage cheese

In a blender or food processor, combine all ingredients except clams. Process until smooth. Blend in clams and chill before serving. Makes 1½ cups.

LIPTAUER CHEESE DIP

2 8-oz. pkgs. cream cheese, softened
¼ c. butter, softened
2 to 3 T. anchovy paste or 4 to 5 anchovy fillets, mashed
½ t. minced onion
1 T. capers, drained
1 t. prepared mustard
⅓ c. milk

Combine all ingredients, mixing well. Chill and shape into a ball. Garnish with minced parsley and serve with crackers. Serves 10 to 12.

SHRIMP DIP

1 3-oz. pkg. cream cheese, softened
½ c. mayonnaise
½ c. snipped green onion (green part only)
1 T. lemon juice
1 dash of Tabasco sauce
1 4½-oz. can of shrimp

Rinse and drain shrimp. Combine all ingredients, mixing well. Chill for several hours before serving. Makes 1½ cups.

SOUR CREAM COTTAGE CHEESE

For calorie watchers.

1 c. creamed cottage cheese
1 T. lemon juice

Combine ingredients in a blender and process until smooth and creamy. May be used in place of yogurt or sour cream in any dip. Makes 1 cup.

JALAPEÑO DIP

2 10-oz. cans jalapeño bean dip
1 T. Worcestershire sauce
1 t. crushed dried chilies (remove seeds)
½ t. cumin
1 lb. grated Monterey Jack cheese

Heat bean dip and seasonings. When steaming hot, add cheese; stir until melted. Serve with corn chips. Makes about 2 cups.

CHILI DIP

½ c. mayonnaise
½ c. sour cream or yogurt
2 T. pickle relish
1 T. chopped stuffed olives
2 t. chili powder
1½ t. grated or minced onion

Combine all ingredients, mixing well. Chill for several hours. Serve with tortilla chips. Makes about 1 cup.

CHESTNUT DIP

16 oz. plain yogurt
1 8-oz. can water chestnuts, drained and chopped
2 T. snipped green onions
1 T. beef-flavored instant bouillon
2 T. snipped parsley
½ t. Worcestershire sauce
¼ t. garlic powder
Dash of Tabasco sauce

Combine all ingredients, mixing well. Chill; stir before serving with assorted fresh vegetables. Makes 2 cups.

BOMBAY DIP

1 c. mayonnaise or salad dressing
2 T. lemon juice
2 t. grated onion
2 t. sugar
1 t. curry powder or more to taste

Combine all ingredients, mixing well. Chill. Serve with raw vegetables. Makes 1 cup.

MOCK GUACAMOLE

Looks like guacamole, but has its own zip.

1 10-oz. pkg. frozen broccoli, cooked, drained
½ c. sour cream
2 T. grated Parmesan cheese
2 T. lemon juice
½ small onion

Place all ingredients in blender; blend until smooth. Serve with corn chips or raw vegetables. Makes about 1½ cups.

BOMBAY DIP (LOW CAL)

2 c. yogurt or sour half and half
4 T. minced fresh parsley or chives
2 T. lemon juice
Sugar substitute to equal 2 t. sugar
2 t. curry powder (or more to taste)

Combine all ingredients, mixing well. Chill. Serve with raw vegetables. Makes about 2 cups.

YOGURT DIP

1 large cucumber
1 c. plain yogurt
⅛ t. garlic powder
⅛ t. dill weed
Salt and white pepper to taste

Peel cucumber, remove seed, grate, and drain. Combine all ingredients and mix well. Chill for several hours before serving. Serve with chips or assorted raw vegetables. Makes 1½ cups.

AVOCADO DIP

1 ripe avocado, peeled and mashed
1 3-oz. pkg. cream cheese, softened
3 T. mayonnaise
Dash of lemon juice
¼ t. garlic powder
Dash of Tabasco

Combine all ingredients, mixing thoroughly. Chill. Serve with vegetables for dipping. Makes about 1 cup.

TUNA DIP

1 8-oz. pkg. cream cheese, softened
¼ c. mayonnaise
1 7-oz. can tuna fish
¼ t. salt
2 t. grated onion
4 to 6 drops Tabasco sauce
½ t. Worcestershire sauce

Rinse and drain tuna; flake. Combine all ingredients. Chill several hours before serving. Makes about 1½ cups.

Eggs

MINIATURE EGG FOO YONG

8 eggs, beaten
1 t. salt
¼ t. pepper
1 c. minced onions
1 c. diced celery
½ c. minced green pepper
1 T. soy sauce
2 c. flaked cooked crab meat, baby shrimp, or diced ham
4 T. vegetable oil

Combine all ingredients except oil; mix well. Heat oil in frying pan; by tablespoons fry small pancakes, browning on both sides. Keep hot in warm oven until ready to serve. Makes 25 pancakes.

FROSTED EGG PATÉ

6 to 8 hard-boiled eggs, minced
6 T. butter, softened
½ t. curry powder
Dash of pepper
¼ c. mayonnaise
Curry powder
Snipped parsley

Combine eggs, butter, curry powder and pepper; mix well. Pat onto a serving plate to ½ to ¾-inch thickness. Chill until firm. Frost with mayonnaise, sprinkle with additional curry powder, and garnish with minced parsley. Serve with toast or crackers. Makes about 1 cup.

CHOPPED EGG APPETIZER

3 to 4 green onions
6 to 8 hard-boiled eggs
¼ c. rendered chicken fat
Salt and freshly ground pepper to taste

Mince green onions, using all of the white and half the green. Finely chop eggs and mix with minced onion. Set aside. To render chicken fat, fry slowly in an ungreased pan. Pour off the fat, let cool. Mix fat with the egg and onion. Season to taste and chill for 2 hours. Serve on lettuce. Makes about 1 cup.

CREAMY EGG DIP

4 hard-boiled eggs, chopped
1 8-oz. pkg. creamed cottage cheese
¾ c. mayonnaise
4 green onions, snipped
Salt and pepper to taste

Combine all ingredients, mixing well. Chill several hours. Serve with seasoned crackers. Makes 2½ cups.

EGG ROLLS

½ c. sifted flour
2 t. cornstarch
¼ t. salt
1 small egg, beaten
½ t. sugar
1 c. water
¼ c. peanut oil
1 T. flour
2 T. water

Sift together flour, cornstarch, and salt. Beat in egg and sugar. Slowly add 1 cup water, beating constantly, until batter is smooth. Lightly grease a hot 6-inch skillet with peanut oil. Pour 3 tablespoons batter into the skillet, tipping to spread batter evenly over bottom. Place over medium heat and fry until batter shrinks from sides of pan. Carefully slide onto a towel to cool. Place 1 tablespoon filling on each egg roll skin on lower section. Fold up and over the filling, away from you. Fold edges toward center. Roll firmly all the way up. Mix 1 tablespoon flour with 2 tablespoons water and brush edges to seal. Heat 1 inch of peanut oil in skillet and fry egg rolls, 2 at a time, until golden. Reheat on a cookie sheet in a 400° oven for 10 to 20 minutes until hot and crispy. Serve with Hot Mustard Sauce. Makes 8 Egg Rolls.

FILLING

¾ c. finely chopped celery
1 c. shredded cabbage
½ c. water
½ c. diced cooked shrimp
½ c. diced pork, ham, chicken, or veal
2 T. peanut oil
¾ c. finely chopped water chestnuts
4 scallions, chopped
1 clove garlic, minced
4 T. soy sauce

In saucepan, combine celery, cabbage, and water; bring to a boil. Drain thoroughly. Heat oil in skillet and sauté shrimp and meat for 2 or 3 minutes. Add remaining ingredients and cook, stirring constantly until lightly browned. Cool.

HOT MUSTARD SAUCE

3 T. dry mustard
Cold water

Stir enough water into mustard to make the consistency of mayonnaise.

STUFFED EGGS

6 hard-boiled eggs
1 7-oz. can tuna, shrimp, salmon or lobster, drained and flaked
½ c. mayonnaise
1 T. minced green onion
2 t. prepared mustard
Salt and pepper to taste

Cut eggs in half lengthwise. Remove yolks and mash. Add remaining ingredients to egg yolks and mix well. Mound mixture into egg white shells and garnish with parsley. Makes 12 Stuffed Eggs.

EGG SALAD MOLD

1½ envelopes gelatin
¼ c. cold water
12 hard-boiled eggs, chopped
½ c. chopped celery
½ c. chopped green pepper
2 t. grated onion
¼ t. white pepper
½ t. Worchestershire sauce
1 c. mayonnaise
2 t. salt
¾ c. hot water
1 1-oz. jar black caviar

Dissolve gelatin in cold water. Add remaining ingredients, except the caviar. Pour into a greased 6-cup mold. Chill until firm. Unmold and serve with bread rounds or crackers. Garnish with black caviar. Makes 12 to 24 servings.

DEVILED EGG BASKETS

1 cucumber, scored and sliced
6 hard-boiled eggs
1 t. prepared horseradish
¼ c. mayonnaise
½ t. prepared mustard

Slice cucumber, seed, and cut each slice in half. Score the slice and set aside to use as a "handle." Cut eggs in half lengthwise. Mash yolks with a fork, blender, or food processor. Add horseradish, mayonnaise, and mustard and beat until smooth. Heap into whites. Top each egg with cucumber slice to make a basket handle. Makes 12 "Baskets."
Note: For variety, add one of the following:
4 T. yogurt
¼ t. salt and dash of white pepper
¼ c. crumbled blue cheese

AVOCADO-FILLED EGGS

6 hard-boiled eggs
1 ripe avocado, mashed
1 t. lemon juice
1 T. olive oil
Salt to taste

Slice hard-boiled eggs in half lengthwise. Remove yolks and mash with an equal amount of mashed avocado. Moisten with lemon juice and olive oil; salt to taste. Heap mixture into each egg white. Sprinkle with paprika and serve chilled. Serves about 6.

HAM AND EGG BALLS

6 hard-boiled eggs, chopped
1 T. minced onion or chives
½ c. ground cooked ham
Dash of pepper
¼ c. mayonnaise
⅔ c. crushed cornflakes or chopped nuts

Combine all ingredients except cornflakes. Shape into small balls. Roll balls in cereal; chill. Makes about 40.

MORE EGG ROLLS

1 c. minced celery
½ c. minced bamboo shoots
½ c. chopped water chestnuts
½ c. shredded celery cabbage or bean sprouts
2 T. thinly sliced green onions
2 T. vegetable oil
1 c. minced cooked shrimp, chicken or turkey
1 T. soy sauce
Dash of pepper
2 c. flour
2¼ c. water
4 eggs

Stir fry vegetables in oil for 3 to 5 minutes. Add shrimp, soy sauce, and pepper; set aside. Combine flour, water, and eggs, mixing well. Heat a 6-inch skillet, brush lightly with oil. Pour about 2 tablespoons batter into skillet, tilting pan quickly to coat bottom. Cook until underside is lightly browned and dry on top. Turn out on tea towel, browned side up. Repeat until batter is used up. Place two tablespoons filling lengthwise on pancake. Fold pancake over filling; fold 1 inch of each side toward center. Roll pancake away from you and seal edge with a dab of beaten egg. Fry 3 or 4 egg rolls at a time in 375° fat until well browned and crisp. Drain on paper toweling. Serve with Mustard and Plum Sauces. Makes about 18.

MUSTARD SAUCE

1 t. dry mustard
1 T. prepared mustard
1 t. lemon juice
1 c. mayonnaise

Combine all ingredients, mixing well.

PLUM SAUCE

1 c. plum preserves
1 T. sugar
1 T. vinegar

Combine all ingredients, mixing well.

EGG AND ANCHOVY SPREAD

3 hard-boiled eggs, minced
2 T. mayonnaise
1 T. anchovy paste
1 t. lemon juice
1 t. snipped green onion

Combine all ingredients, mixing well. Makes about 1 cup.

ANCHOVY EGGS

12 hard-boiled eggs, halved
½ to ¾ c. mayonnaise
2 cans rolled anchovies with capers, drained

Mash egg yolks; blend in mayonnaise. Fill egg whites with yolk mixture and top each with an anchovy. Makes 24.

ANCHOVY STUFFED EGGS

6 hard-boiled eggs
⅓ c. yogurt or sour cream
2 T. anchovy paste
1 T. snipped scallions
Minced fresh parsley

Cut eggs in half lengthwise and remove the yolks. Mash with a fork, blending in the yogurt, anchovy paste, and onions. Fill whites with mixture. Sprinkle with minced fresh parsley and chill before serving. Makes 12 appetizers.
Note: For a variation, omit anchovy paste and garnish filled egg with caviar.

HAM AND EGG BOATS

12 hard-boiled eggs, peeled
1 c. minced ham
½ c. mayonnaise
½ small onion, minced
1 T. mustard
12 thin rounds sweet pickle, cut in half

Cut eggs in half lengthwise. Mash egg yolks; combine with ham, mayonnaise, onion, and mustard. Heap into egg white halves. Garnish with pickle slice. Makes 24.

CAVIAR A LA RUSSE

6 eggs, hard-boiled and chopped
4 T. butter, melted
1 t. minced onion or onion flakes
½ c. sour cream or sour cream substitute
1 4-oz. jar red or black caviar

Combine chopped eggs, butter, and onion. Spread on an 8-inch dessert or salad plate. Chill until firm. Frost with sour cream. Chill again. Just before serving, top with caviar. Cut into wedges and serve with toast or crackers. Serves 4 to 6.

CAVIAR EGGS

6 hard-boiled eggs
1 2-oz. jar small red caviar, drained
2 t. minced onion
¾ c. sour cream

Cut eggs lengthwise in half. Remove yolks. Mash only half of the yolks, adding onion and 1 tablespoon of the sour cream. Save the remaining half of the yolks for use elsewhere. Reserve 1 teaspoon of caviar for garnish; stir remaining caviar into the yolk mixture. Fill eggs. Frost top of eggs with sour cream and garnish each with 2 caviar eggs. Arrange with parsley on a serving dish. Makes 12 Caviar Eggs.

Pictured opposite:
Caviar Eggs

Meat, Poultry, and Cold Cuts

BROILED GROUND BEEF TRIANGLES

4 to 5 slices of bread, toasted on 1 side
Softened butter
Prepared mustard
½ lb. ground round
¼ c. milk
½ t. salt
½ t. pepper
1 T. instant minced onion

Spread untoasted side of bread with butter and then lightly with mustard. Combine meat, milk, salt, pepper, and onion. Spread on top of mustard to the edges of bread. Broil, meat side up, 5 to 7 minutes until meat is done. Cut each sandwich into 4 triangles. Makes 16 to 20 triangles.

MINI HAMBURGERS

3 doz. miniature hamburger buns
1 lb. ground round steak
1 T. chili sauce
1 small onion, minced
1 clove garlic, minced
1 T. mustard
Sliced cheese, optional

Combine all ingredients, except hamburger buns. Spread round steak mixture on buns. Top with sliced cheese, if desired. Bake in a 400° oven for 30 minutes or until meat is no longer pink. Makes 3 dozen Mini Hamburgers.

BEEF TARTARE

1 lb. twice ground top round or sirloin steak, fat removed
1 egg yolk
1 t. salt
1 t. Worcestershire sauce or steak sauce
Dash of Tabasco sauce
1 T. minced onion
½ t. freshly ground pepper
1 t. capers, drained
4 anchovy fillets, for top of meat
Pimiento-stuffed olives
Cherry tomatoes
Onion rings

Gently combine all ingredients, except olives, tomatoes and onion rings. Shape into flattened circle; refrigerate. Just before serving, place on a platter. Top with anchovy strips and ring with olives, tomatoes, and onion rings. Serve with thin slices of pumpernickel or rye bread. Serves 6 to 8.

BEEF SANDWICHES

36 party rye slices, buttered
Very thin slices of roast beef
1 c. mayonnaise
2 T. horseradish
2 T. brown mustard

Top buttered bread with sliced beef. Combine remaining ingredients. Garnish sandwiches with a dollop of sauce. Makes 36 open-faced sandwiches.

DRIED BEEF PINWHEELS

1 3-oz. pkg. cream cheese, softened
2 T. snipped green onions
1 t. garlic powder or seasoning salt
1 to 2 T. mayonnaise
¼ lb. sliced dried beef

Mix cheese, onions, garlic powder, and mayonnaise together. Spread 2 slices of beef with mixture and place one on top of the other. Roll up tightly and chill several hours or overnight. Cut each roll into 1½ to 2-inch slices; insert a toothpick into edge of each slice. Makes about 36.

HOT CHIPPED BEEF ROLLS

1 8-oz. pkg. chipped beef
1 3-oz. pkg. cream cheese, softened with 1 T. mayonnaise
1 T. minced onion
1 loaf thinly sliced bread, crusts removed
Butter or margarine, softened

Mix beef with cheese and onion. Spread bread slices with butter or margarine. Turn over and spread with beef cheese mixture. Roll up and secure with toothpick. Place on baking sheet; bake in a 325° oven until golden brown. Serve warm. Makes 3 to 4 dozen.

BAR-B-Q BEEF BUNS

1 onion, chopped
1 T. butter
1 c. catsup
½ c. water
¼ c. vinegar
1 T. Worchestershire sauce
1 t. sugar
Dash of salt
Cocktail buns

In a saucepan sauté onion in butter until tender; add remaining ingredients and simmer for 10 to 15 minutes. Warm thinly sliced roast beef, brisket, or chicken in sauce. Place in cocktail buns. Makes enough for 3 to 4 dozen sandwiches.

TURKISH MEATBALLS WITH YOGURT

4 slices thin white bread, crusts trimmed, torn into 1-inch pieces
⅓ c. water
½ lb. ground lamb
¼ c. minced onion
½ t. salt
¼ t. ground cumin
¼ t. pepper
¼ c. flour
Vegetable oil
1 c. yogurt

Soak bread in water until most of the water is absorbed. Squeeze out excess water. Combine all ingredients except flour, oil, and yogurt. Shape rounded teaspoons of mixture into balls. Roll each in flour. Fry in 1 inch of hot oil until golden. Drain on paper toweling. May be reheated in 350° oven until hot (about 20 minutes). Serve on toothpicks around a bowl of yogurt mixed with snipped parsley, mint, and salt. Makes 18 to 24 meatballs.

MEATBALLS MADRAS

2 eggs, beaten
1 c. chopped mixed dried fruits (apricots, prunes, raisins, apples)
½ c. finely chopped onion
½ c. crumbled fresh bread crumbs
1½ t. salt
1 dash of Tabasco sauce
1½ lbs. ground beef (may contain veal and pork)
2 T. vegetable oil or margarine
1 c. sweet vermouth

Combine all ingredients, except oil and vermouth, until evenly mixed. Shape into 1-inch balls. In a large skillet, sauté 1 layer of meatballs at a time in hot oil until evenly browned. Place in a heated chafing dish. Warm vermouth; pour over all, and serve. Makes about 50 meatballs.

SWEDISH MEATBALLS

1 lb. ground round
½ c. fine dry bread crumbs
½ c. milk
1 egg, slightly beaten
1 t. salt
½ t. nutmeg
    Dash of pepper
2 T. Worcestershire sauce
3 T. flour
½ t. salt
2 c. light cream *plus* ½ c. milk
2 T. vegetable oil

Mix together first eight ingredients. Shape into 1-inch meatballs. Heat oil in a frying pan and sauté half of the meatballs until browned. Continue to cook until meatballs are done. Repeat with remaining meatballs. Blend flour and ½ teaspoon salt into drippings in frying pan. Gradually blend in cream and milk. Stir until thickened and comes to a boil. Mix in meatballs; heat through. Makes 60 to 80 meatballs.

MEATBALLS

1 lb. ground beef
¼ lb. pork sausage, cooked and drained
2 eggs, beaten
½ c. fine bread crumbs
1 can mincemeat pie filling
½ to 1 c. apple cider
1 T. wine vinegar

Combine meats, eggs, and crumbs. Mix well and form into 5 to 6 dozen tiny meatballs. Bake in a 375° oven for 15 to 20 minutes. Cool and drain. At serving time, combine pie filling, cider, and vinegar. Pour over meatballs and heat. Serve hot. Makes 5 to 6 dozen meatballs.

MEDITERRANEAN MEATBALLS

1 lb. ground beef
1 c. cooked rice
⅓ c. minced onion
¼ c. snipped fresh dill
¼ c. snipped fresh parsley
1 egg, beaten
1 t. salt
⅛ t. pepper
½ c. flour
1 egg, beaten
    Vegetable oil

Combine first 8 ingredients; mix until smooth. Shape meat into balls and dip in flour, then egg. Heat 1 inch of oil in skillet; fry meatballs until golden. Makes 30 meatballs.

CHAFING DISH MEATBALLS

1½ lbs. ground round
½ c. diced bread crumbs
1 t. salt
¼ t. pepper
1 egg, slightly beaten
½ c. milk
2 T. vegetable oil
1 1-lb. 4-oz. can pineapple chunks, drained
1 17-oz. jar stuffed olives or 1 green pepper cut in chunks

Toss together ground round, bread crumbs, salt, pepper, egg, and milk until well blended. Shape into ¾-inch balls and chill for 2 hours. Bake meatballs in a shallow pan with oil in a 350° oven for 30 minutes. Drain all fat, cover with sauce and bake an additional 30 minutes. Spoon into chafing dish with pineapple chunks, green olives or green pepper chunks. Makes about 48 meatballs.

SAUCE

1 bottle chili sauce
1 bottle water
1 small jar of grape jelly

Combine all ingredients and bring to a boil.

Pictured opposite:
Chafing Dish Meatballs

BARBECUED SPARERIBS

2 lbs. spareribs, cut in bite-size pieces
½ c. brown sugar
1 c. catsup
¼ c. soy sauce
¼ t. cumin
2 T. sherry
2 T. vinegar

Combine all ingredients except spareribs, mixing well. Marinate ribs 3 to 4 hours in sauce. Remove and bake, covered, in a 300° oven for 1½ hours. Remove cover, add sauce; bake and baste 1 hour longer. Makes 8 to 10 servings.

MOCK PATÉ DE FOIS GRAS

4 to 5 large mushrooms, sliced
2 T. butter
½ lb. liverwurst, mashed
1 3-oz. pkg. cream cheese, softened
1 T. Worcestershire sauce
½ t. thyme
¼ c. heavy cream

Sauté mushrooms in butter. Mix together all ingredients. Chill; serve with crackers or pumpernickel bread. Serves 4 to 6.

TURKEY ROLL-UPS

¼ c. mayonnaise
¼ t. curry powder
12 thin slices turkey
12 green pepper strips
12 Swiss cheese strips

Mix together mayonnaise and curry powder. Lightly spread each turkey slice with mayonnaise mixture. Place a green pepper strip and a Swiss cheese strip at one end of turkey slice. Roll up turkey jelly-roll fashion; secure with 2 toothpicks. Cut Turkey Roll-Up in half. Makes 24.

CHINESE RIBS

2 lbs. spareribs
½ c. soy sauce
3 T. catsup
1 T. dry sherry
1 T. brown sugar
½ t. ginger
¼ t. garlic powder
2 T. honey

Combine soy sauce, catsup, sherry, brown sugar, ginger, and garlic powder in pan large enough to hold ribs. In a separate cup combine honey with 1 tablespoon soy sauce marinade and set aside. Coat spareribs with soy sauce marinade; marinate for at least 1 hour, turning occasionally. Place ribs on a broiler pan; bake in a 350° oven for 1 to 1½ hours brushing frequently with marinade. During the last five minutes, brush ribs with the honey mixture. Serve hot. Makes 6 to 8 servings.

TURKEY SANDWICHES

¼ c. butter, softened
1 T. mustard
1 t. horseradish
36 fingers of thin white bread
Thin slices of turkey breast

Combine butter, mustard, and horseradish. Spread bread with seasoned butter; top with turkey. Makes 3 dozen fingers.

CURRIED CHICKEN OR TURKEY

2 c. minced cooked chicken or turkey
½ to ¾ c. mayonnaise
¼ c. minced celery
1 to 2 t. curry powder
4 to 6 dozen Crustades, p. 6

Mix all ingredients together. Serve in crustades with minced parsley or snipped chives on top. Makes 3 cups.

BAKED CHICKEN PATÉ

1 medium onion, chopped
1 clove garlic, minced
2 eggs
1 lb. chicken livers
¼ c. flour
½ t. allspice
1 t. salt
½ t. pepper
¼ c. butter
1 c. light cream

Place all ingredients in a blender; blend until smooth. Pour into a greased 1-quart baking dish; cover. Set in pan of hot water and bake in a 325° oven for 3 hours. Cool, then chill. Unmold and serve with unsalted crackers or melba toast.

CHICKEN SALAD SPREAD

2 c. cooked chicken, minced
¼ c. celery, minced
½ c. mayonnaise
2 T. sour cream
1 T. sherry
1 T. lemon juice
    Ripe olives, sliced, for garnish
    Paprika

Mix all together. Serve garnished with ripe olive slices and sprinkled with paprika. Makes about 2 cups.

CHICKEN LIVERS CANTON

1 to 2 lbs. chicken livers, fresh or frozen, thawed
1 c. soy sauce
¼ c. butter
¼ c. flour

Cover chicken livers with soy sauce and marinate overnight in the refrigerator. Drain well; dust with flour. Sauté in butter for about 5 minutes until no longer pink. Shake pan occasionally to brown livers on all sides. Serve with toothpicks. Makes 10 to 12 servings.

CHICKEN OR TURKEY SOUFFLÉS

2 c. minced chicken or turkey
1 3-oz. pkg. cream cheese, softened
½ c. mayonnaise
1 T. lemon juice
1 T. capers
    Dash of Tabasco
    Toast rounds

Mix all together. Mound onto toast rounds and broil until puffy. Makes 2 to 3 dozen.

CHICKEN SPREAD

2 c. finely chopped chicken or turkey (dark meat)
½ c. chopped ripe olives
    Salt and pepper to taste
    Mayonnaise to bind

Combine all ingredients, mixing well. Spread on choice of breads or toast. Serves 12 to 16.

SESAME SEED CHICKEN WINGS
BATTER

2 eggs
¾ c. flour
½ t. salt
¾ c. cold water

Beat eggs; gradually add flour and salt. Add water slowly and beat until smooth and thin. Refrigerate for 30 minutes. Remove from refrigerator 30 minutes before using.

12 to 16 chicken wings, discard tips
½ c. sesame seed
4 c. peanut or corn oil

Heat oil to 375° in skillet or deep fryer. Dip each chicken wing in batter; sprinkle with sesame seed. Deep fry four wings at a time for 10 to 12 minutes, turning several times. Remove from oil and drain on paper toweling. Repeat until all pieces are fried. Serve with bottled sweet sour sauce, if desired. Serves 6 to 12.

CHICKEN WINGS, MEXICANA

32 chicken wings
1 T. vegetable oil
1½ c. diced onion
1½ c. diced green and red pepper
1½ c. diced canned tomatoes
1½ T. tomato paste
2 cloves garlic, minced
1 t. salt
¼ t. pepper
¼ t. chili powder
½ envelope beef onion soup mix *or*
1 c. brown gravy mix

Sauté onion in oil until soft. Combine all ingredients and pour over chicken. Place in a baking dish. Bake in a 375° oven for 30 to 45 minutes until tender. Serve hot in sauce.

CHICKEN WINGS

32 chicken wings
⅔ c. melted butter
1 t. salt
½ t. garlic powder
1½ c. bread crumbs
½ c. grated Parmesan cheese

Discard wing tips; cut remaining wing into 2 pieces. Season melted butter with salt and garlic powder. Combine bread crumbs and grated cheese, stirring to mix well. Dip wings in butter, then in crumb-cheese mixture. Place on a 15 x 10-inch baking sheet; bake in a 400° oven for 30 minutes. Makes 32 appetizers.

HAWAIIAN KABOBS

1 lb. bologna, cut into 24 cubes
24 pineapple cubes
2 T. soy sauce
1 T. brown sugar
1 T. vinegar

Spear cubes of meat and pineapple on toothpick. Place on broil-and-serve platter. Brush with combined mixture of soy sauce, sugar, and vinegar. Broil, turning, until hot and golden. Makes 24.

FRANKLY HAWAIIAN

Cocktail wieners or frankfurters cut in
  1-inch pieces
1 c. brown sugar
2 t. mustard
3 T. flour
1 c. pineapple juice
½ c. vinegar
1 T. soy sauce

Combine all ingredients, except wieners; heat, stirring until sauce comes to a boil. Add wieners and heat through. Serve in a chafing dish. Makes 4 to 5 dozen.

STIK & PIK

HOT KABOBS

With toothpicks, alternate pineapple chunks or pickled onions with one of the following and then broil:

Ham cubes
Cooked shrimp
Scallops
1-inch frankfurter pieces
Chicken livers

COLD KABOBS

Using toothpick, carrot or celery stick, alternate 2 or more of the following:

Melon balls
Pineapple chunks
Cold meat cubes
Chicken cubes
Cooked shrimp
Cheese cubes
Wiener chunks, cubed salami, cut in
  1-inch pieces
Cubes of pickle
Cherry tomatoes
Cubes of cheese
Pickled onion
Stuffed green olive
Orange slices
Ham cubes
Canned mushroom
Radishes

HAM AND SWISS SQUARES

12 slices boiled ham
2 8-oz. pkgs. Swiss cheese spread, softened
2 T. hot mustard
½ c. minced parsley

Mix together cheese, mustard and parsley. Spread half the mixture on 4 slices of ham, top with another slice of ham, then spread remaining cheese, and top with remaining ham. Chill for ½ hour. Cut into bite-sized cubes. Dip edges in minced parsley. Makes about 3 dozen.

HAM SPREAD

1 c. chopped ham
¼ c. finely grated Cheddar cheese
1 t. prepared mustard
2 t. pickle relish
3 T. mayonnaise

Combine all ingredients, mixing well. Serve on toast or crackers. Makes 1⅓ cups.

BACON STICKS

12 unsalted bread sticks
12 slices bacon

Wrap each bread stick, spiral fashion, with a bacon slice. Bake in a 400° oven for 10 to 12 minutes until bacon is crisp. Makes 12 sticks.

SALAMI TRIANGLES

1 8-oz. pkg. cream cheese, softened
2 T. prepared horseradish
¼ t. Tabasco sauce
36 slices salami

Blend cheese with horseradish and Tabasco sauce. Spread 12 slices of salami with the cheese mixture. Top with another slice of salami, more cheese and a third slice of salami. Cut each circle into quarters; spear each with a toothpick. Makes 48 triangles.

ZIPPY HAM SPREAD

2 c. ground ham
2 T. prepared mustard
2 T. horseradish
1 c. sour cream

Blend all ingredients together, mixing well. Serve with rye or pumpernickel bread. Makes about 3 cups.

DEVILED HAM SPREAD

2 cans deviled ham
2 hard-boiled eggs, minced
½ small onion, minced
1 T. minced sweet pickle
½ c. mayonnaise

Mix all ingredients together, blending well. Serve with party rye or crackers. Makes about 1 cup.

BACON BALLS

Stuffed green olives
Bacon slices

Wrap stuffed olive in ¼ to ½ of a bacon slice. Broil until bacon is done. Serve on toothpicks.

LIVER SAUSAGE SPREAD

1 8-oz. pkg. cream cheese, softened
1 8-oz. pkg. liver sausage or Braunschweiger
1 T. minced onion
2 t. lemon juice
1 t. Worcestershire sauce
Salt and pepper to taste

Blend all ingredients together, mixing well. Garnish with parsley; serve with crackers. Makes 2 cups.

TOASTED BRAUNSCHWEIGER

Braunschweiger or liver sausage
Bread rounds
Butter
Mustard
Grated onion
Stuffed olives, sliced

Butter bread rounds and spread with a little mustard. Mix braunschweiger and onion; spread thickly on top of butter. Broil for about 5 to 7 minutes until hot. Garnish with sliced olive. Serve hot.

BUFFET BAR-B-Q

1 large cabbage, red or green
1 small can sterno
Cocktail sausages
Shrimp
Chunks of bologna and salami

Cut off slice from bottom of cabbage. Hollow out space in the top of cabbage to hold small container of sterno. Stud the cabbage with toothpick speared sausages and shrimp. Guests grill their own. Serve with sauce.

BARBECUE SAUCE

1 c. catsup
½ c. chili sauce
2 T. prepared horseradish
1 t. Worcestershire sauce
¼ t. Tabasco sauce

Combine all ingredients, mixing well. Heat and serve.

PICK-EM-UPS

Cocktail Prunes
Remove pits from extra large prunes. Fill with one of the following:

Sharp cheese spread
Peanut butter mixed with crisp bacon
Ham and cream cheese spread
Cream cheese mixed with chopped nuts
Whole blanched almond

COCKTAIL SAUSAGES

Cocktail wieners or frankfurters cut in 1-inch pieces
¼ c. mustard
½ c. currant jelly

Heat mustard and jelly in a saucepan. Add wieners and heat, covered, about 10 minutes. Serve in a chafing dish. Makes 2 to 3 dozen.

MEAT ROLL-UPS

8 thin slices of cooked meat:
Salami
Spiced ham
Bologna
Dried beef
Boiled ham
Roast beef
Turkey ham

Spread filling on meat slices and roll up tightly. Chill thoroughly; cut into bite-sized pieces, or shape each slice into a cone. Makes 30 to 36.

FILLING

4 oz. cream cheese
Grated onion
Worcestershire sauce or mustard
Horseradish
Tabasco

Combine all ingredients according to taste; mix together well.
Note: For variation, use any prepared cheese spread.

Pastries

ROQUEFORT ROLL-UPS

1 8-oz. pkg. cream cheese
1 8-oz. pkg. Roquefort or blue cheese
½ c. mayonnaise
1 T. Worcestershire sauce
2 T. minced onion
1 c. butter, melted
 Loaf of thinly sliced sandwich bread, crusts removed

Mix together cheeses and seasonings. Spread on bread slices, roll up jelly-roll fashion; dip in melted butter and bake on a cookie sheet in a 350° oven for 15 to 18 minutes. Cool slightly and cut into thirds. Makes 4 to 6 dozen.

MINIATURE CREPES

2 eggs
1 c. water
⅔ c. flour
½ t. salt
2 T. melted butter
½ pt. sour cream
1 2½ to 4-oz. jar red or black caviar

Beat eggs with half of the water. Stir in flour and salt. Add remaining water and butter. Spoon into a hot greased frying pan, making crepes paper thin and not more than 3 inches in diameter. Spread with sour cream and caviar; roll up. To serve, heat in a 300° oven for 3 to 5 minutes until just warm. Makes 36 crepes.

ARTICHOKE BALLS

¼ c. butter
1 small onion, minced
1 15-oz. can artichoke hearts, drained and minced
1 clove garlic, minced
½ c. grated Parmesan cheese
½ c. toasted bread crumbs
½ t. salt

Melt butter; sauté onion, artichoke, and garlic until onion is shiny. Remove from heat. Add cheese, salt, and bread crumbs to artichoke mixture. Form into 3 to 4 dozen bite-size balls. Bake in a 300° oven for 8 to 10 minutes. Makes 3 to 4 dozen Artichoke Balls.

QUICHE FOR A CROWD

2 cans green chiles
1 20-oz. pkg. Muenster or Monterey Jack cheese, diced
6 eggs, beaten
12 crackers, crushed
1 c. sour half and half

Rinse chiles, remove seeds, drain, and chop. Mix all ingredients together. Pour into a greased 11 x 13-inch casserole. Bake in a 350° oven for 50 to 60 minutes until bubbly and slightly brown. Remove from oven; cool for 15 minutes. Cut into 1-inch squares and serve warm. Serves 4 to 6.

MINIATURE QUICHE

2 c. flour
1 8-oz. pkg. sharp Cheddar cheese, grated
½ lb. margarine or butter
Dash of cayenne

Cream together cheese, butter and cayenne. Add flour and mix into a smooth dough. Wrap and chill for an hour or freeze for 30 minutes. Then form into 48 1-inch balls and press into miniature muffin tins. Place ½ teaspoon filling in center of each quiche then 1 tablespoon custard. Bake in a 400° oven for 12 to 15 minutes. Cool 5 minutes and remove from tins. Serve warm. You may freeze and reheat. Makes 48 Quiche.

CUSTARD MIX

4 eggs
1 c. milk
2 T. flour *plus* ¼ t. salt

Mix together well.

DENVER FILLING

1 c. chopped salami
½ onion, minced
1 T. butter

Sauté onion in butter. Stir in salami.

MUSHROOM FILLING

1 4-oz. can mushrooms, sliced
½ onion, minced
1 T. butter

Sauté mushrooms and onion in butter.

SHRIMP 'N CHEESE FILLING

48 baby shrimp
4 oz. of blue cheese crumbled

Mix together well.

SPINACH FILLING

1 pkg. frozen chopped spinach
½ onion, minced
1 T. butter

Cook spinach; drain well. Sauté onion in butter; stir in spinach.

ARTICHOKE SQUARES

2 jars marinated artichoke hearts, chopped
1 bunch green onions, sliced
2 T. vegetable oil
1 clove garlic, minced
1 c. grated Cheddar cheese
½ t. Worcestershire sauce
¼ t. Tabasco sauce
4 eggs, beaten
½ c. crushed soda crackers
Minced parsley

Drain the artichoke hearts, saving the oil. Sauté onion in oil. Combine all ingredients except crackers and parsley; put into a greased 8-inch square pan. Sprinkle with cracker crumbs and parsley. Bake in a 325° oven for 35 to 40 minutes. Chill for several hours. Cut into small squares and serve. Makes sixteen 2 x 2-inch squares.

PIZZA HORNS

1¼ c. flour
¼ t. salt
⅓ c. yogurt or sour cream
3 T. melted margarine
1 lb. lean ground beef
1 T. minced onion
½ c. pizza sauce
¼ t. oregano
1 T. minced parsley
1 egg, slightly beaten

Stir yogurt and margarine into flour and salt. On a lightly floured surface, knead gently to form a smooth dough. Add more flour if needed. Cover and let rest 30 minutes. Sauté meat and onion until browned; drain. Add pizza sauce, oregano, and parsley and stir; cool. Divide dough into thirds. Roll out each third to a 9-inch circle. Cut each circle into 8 triangles. Place a heaping teaspoon of pizza filling on the wide end of each triangle. Roll up each triangle from the wide end. Brush each triangle with slightly beaten egg. Prick tops with fork. Bake in a 400° oven for 10 to 12 minutes or until golden brown. Serve hot. Makes 24.

SESAME PUFFS

1 c. water
½ c. butter or margarine
½ t. salt
1¼ c. flour
4 eggs
⅓ c. sour cream
¼ c. sesame seed
1 lb. ground smoked ham
1 T. dill weed
¼ c. mayonnaise
1 T. mustard

Bring water, butter, and salt to a boil. Remove from heat and add flour all at once. Stir with a wooden spoon until mixture forms a ball. Add eggs, one at a time, beating well after each addition. Add sour cream and sesame seed, beating until smooth. Drop dough by rounded tablespoons onto a greased cookie sheet. Bake in a 425° oven for 12 minutes. Prick each puff with a fork and continue baking for 3 more minutes. Remove from cookie sheets and cool on wire racks. Combine remaining ingredients, adding more mayonnaise if necessary. Cut slice off top of each puff and remove any soft dough inside. Fill with ham mixture, or any filling of your choice. Replace tops and chill until serving time. Makes about 30.

TIROPETAS

½ lb. Feta cheese, crumbled
1 6 to 8-oz. pkg. cottage cheese
⅛ t. salt
3 eggs
2 pkgs. frozen chopped spinach, thawed and drained (optional)
1 t. minced onion (optional)
½ t. nutmeg (optional)
¼ lb. butter, melted
1 lb. phylo dough (20 sheets)
1 T. chopped parsley

Blend cheeses well. Add eggs, salt, parsley and optional ingredients, if desired. Working with 1 sheet of dough at a time, while keeping remainder refrigerated and covered with a dampened towel, cut phylo dough lengthwise into 2-inch strips. Brush strips with melted butter. Place 1 teaspoon of filling at end of strip, folding over end to make a triangle. Continue folding strip from side to side forming triangles, until all is folded. Place seam side down on a baking sheet. Brush tops with melted butter and bake in a 400° oven for 10 to 15 minutes until golden brown. May be frozen unbaked. Makes abut 10 dozen.

CHEESY TOMATO BREAD

1 large loaf of French bread, sliced in half lengthwise
Butter, softened
1 8-oz. can tomato sauce
Salt and pepper
¼ t. garlic powder
¼ t. basil
¼ t. oregano
2 c. grated Mozzarella cheese
1 c. grated Parmesan cheese

Butter cut surfaces of bread; spread with tomato sauce. Top with mixed seasonings. Sprinkle with Mozzarella, then with Parmesan. Place on baking sheet and bake in a 350° oven for 8 to 10 minutes. Cut bread diagonally into 1½-inch thick slices; serve hot. Serves 8 to 12.

PUFFED SHRIMP

1 egg white
Salt
⅓ c. mayonnaise
1 T. finely chopped celery
2 t. chopped chives
½ t. prepared mustard
¼ t. cream-style horseradish
1 4½-oz. can shrimp, drained and rinsed
16 squares of bread, buttered

Beat egg white with dash of salt until soft peaks form. Fold in all ingredients except the shrimp. Spread bread with egg white mixture and top each slice with a shrimp. Bake on an ungreased cookie sheet in a 375° oven for 8 to 10 minutes. Serve warm. Makes 16.

HERB TOAST

1 loaf thin sliced bread, cut into squares or fingers
½ c. butter, melted
¼ t. dill
¼ t. basil
¼ t. thyme
¼ t. marjoram

Add seasonings to butter. Dip bread pieces into butter. Bake in a 300° oven for 20 to 30 minutes until crisp and brown. Store covered. Makes 4 squares or 3 triangles per slice of bread.

PARMESAN CHEESE CRACKERS

¾ c. grated Parmesan cheese
¾ c. margarine or butter, softened
½ t. salt
1½ c. flour
¾ c. chopped walnuts

Cream together cheese and margarine. Add flour and salt; mix to form dough. Blend in nuts. Form into 2 rolls about 1 inch in diameter. Roll in waxed paper; refrigerate for one hour. Slice into thin wafers and bake on an ungreased cookie sheet in a 350° oven for 12 to 15 minutes. Sprinkle lightly with salt while warm. Makes 4 to 6 dozen.

CANADIAN BACON PASTIES

6 frozen patty shells, thawed
6 slices Canadian bacon, cut ¼-inch thick
6 slices Swiss or Cheddar cheese
Prepared mustard

On lightly floured surface, roll each shell to a 9-inch circle. Spread bacon with mustard and top with cheese slice. Moisten edges of patty shell and fold two opposite sides to center, overlapping a little. Then fold other two sides to center, pinching edges to seal. Repeat 5 more times. Prick tops. Place on ungreased baking sheet. Bake in a 400° oven for 20 to 25 minutes or until golden. Makes 6 pasties.

MINIATURE CREAM PUFFS

½ c. water
¼ c. butter or margarine
⅛ t. salt
½ c. flour
¼ c. finely grated Cheddar cheese (optional)
2 eggs

Combine water and butter in a saucepan; bring to a boil. Add salt and flour all at once; stir quickly until mixture forms a ball. Remove from heat. Add cheese, if desired. Beat in 1 egg at a time, beating well until mixture is like velvet. Refrigerate mixture for 1 hour. Place 1 scant teaspoonful on a lightly greased cookie sheet; mound with tip of spoon. Bake in a 400° oven for 15 to 18 minutes until puffed and golden brown. Split cream puffs in half and fill with desired filling. Makes abut 4 to 5 dozen.

MEAT FILLING

1½ c. chopped cooked chicken, shrimp, or crab meat
2 T. minced celery or water chestnuts
1 t. minced onion
Seasoned salt to taste
3 to 4 T. mayonnaise

Combine all ingredients, mixing well; fill puffs.

CUCUMBER FILLING

1 c. chopped cucumber
1 3-oz. pkg. cream cheese, softened
½ t. grated onion
½ t. salt
Dash of pepper
2 to 3 T. mayonnaise

Combine all ingredients, mixing well; fill puffs.

CREAM CHEESE AND OLIVE FILLING

1 8-oz. pkg. cream cheese
½ t. instant chicken bouillion
1 T. minced onion
½ c. chopped ripe olives
2 T. mayonnaise

Combine all ingredients mixing well; fill puffs.

*Pictured opposite:
Miniature Cream Puffs*

MUSHROOM TURNOVERS

1 8-oz. pkg. cream cheese, softened
1 c. margarine or butter
2 c. flour
4 4-oz. cans of mushrooms, minced, and
   drained
½ onion, minced
3 T. butter
2 T. flour
¼ t. salt
¼ t. pepper
1 T. dry sherry
¼ c. sour cream

Cream together cheese and butter; add flour and form into a dough. Divide into 3 balls. Wrap each in waxed paper and chill at least 1 hour. Sauté mushrooms and onion in butter. Stir in flour, salt, pepper, and sherry. Cook until well blended. Remove from heat. Stir in sour cream and allow mixture to cool. Roll dough to a ⅛-inch thickness on lightly floured board. Cut out 3-inch circles. Place 1 teaspoon of filling on each, fold in half, stretching dough and crimping the edges. Bake in a 375° oven for 15 to 20 minutes until golden brown. Before baking, brush each with an egg wash of 1 egg yolk mixed with 1 tablespoon water. Makes about 40 to 48 turnovers.

BLUE CHEESE WEDGES

English muffins, split in half
Butter or margarine
Blue cheese crumbled

Spread muffin halves with butter; sprinkle with crumbled blue cheese and broil until bubbly. Cut into wedges.

MUSHROOM BALLS

1 8-oz. pkg. cream cheese
¼ lb. butter or margarine
1 c. flour
   Pinch of salt
1 lb. fresh firm mushroom caps, washed
   and dried
   Butter
   Salt, pepper, and garlic powder to taste
1 egg, beaten

Cream together cheese and butter until well blended. Add flour and salt; mix well to form a dough. Chill for 1 hour. Sauté mushroom buttons, rounded sides down first, in small amount of hot butter. Turn over and brown second side. Don't cook more than 2 to 3 minutes. Season with salt, pepper, and garlic powder. Let cool.

Roll out dough to 9 x 12-inches and cut into 3-inch squares. Place mushrooms on each piece of dough and enclose, pinching ends, and rolling gently to form a ball. Place balls on lightly greased baking sheet and brush with beaten egg. Bake in a 425° oven for 20 minutes or until golden brown. Makes about 24.

HAM PINWHEELS

1½ c. flour
 1 c. grated Cheddar cheese
 ½ c. butter, softened
 2 T. water
 8 thin slices cooked ham
 ½ c. minced onion
 ¼ c. milk

Mix together flour, cheese, butter and water until dough forms. Divide dough into 2 equal balls. Roll each ball into a 10 x 14-inch rectangle. Cut each rectangle into four 5 x 7-inch pieces. Place 1 slice ham on each rectangle; sprinkle with minced onion. Roll jelly-roll fashion. Place each roll on a cookie sheet; brush with milk. Bake in a 450° oven for 10 to 12 minutes until golden brown. Remove and cut each roll into 4 or 5 pinwheels. Serve hot. Makes 32 to 40 Ham Pinwheels.

CROSTINI

1 loaf thin-sliced bread, slightly stale
Butter

Cut bread slices into 2-inch squares or circles. In a frying pan, melt butter and brown bread on 1 side only. Before serving, spread the untoasted side with 1 of the following spreads:

ANCHOVY AND MOZZARELLA

8 thin slices of Mozzarella cheese, cut into 1-inch squares
8 anchovy fillets

Place cheese on crostini; lay anchovy fillet on top of cheese. Broil on baking sheet 4 inches from heat for 1 minute or until cheese is golden. Makes 8.

ANCHOVY AND OLIVES

1 can anchovies, drained
3 pimiento-stuffed olives

Finely chop olives and anchovies. Blend well. Spread on crostini. Makes 8.

ANCHOVY AND PARMESAN

1 can anchovy fillets with capers, drained
2 T. Parmesan cheese, grated
2 t. lemon juice

Mash anchovy fillets to a paste. Add cheese and lemon juice, mixing well. Spread on crostini. Makes 6 to 12.

ANCHOVY AND TUNA

1 can tuna fish
3 anchovies, chopped
1 T. lemon juice
2 T. tomato paste
Dash of Tabasco sauce

Combine all ingredients, blending well. Spread on crostini. Makes 12 to 20.

PIGS-IN-A-BLANKET

1 can crescent roll dough
2 T. mustard
2 T. pickle relish, drained (optional)
24 cocktail wieners

Separate 1 can of dough into 8 triangles. Spread with mustard and relish. Cut each triangle into 3 small triangles. Place a wiener on the wide end of each triangle. Roll up and place on an ungreased cookie sheet. Bake in a 375° oven for 10 to 12 minutes. Serve hot. Makes 24.

SPICY BISCUITS

1 lb. sharp Cheddar cheese, grated
1 lb. hot bulk sausage
3 c. biscuit mix

Melt cheese in top of a double boiler. Add sausage; stir until sausage is thoroughly cooked. Add to biscuit mix; blend well. Form into 1-inch balls. Bake in a 450° oven for 15 to 20 minutes. Makes 3 to 4 dozen.

CHEESE BALLS

1 5-oz. jar sharp Cheddar cheese spread
¼ c. butter
½ t. salt
½ c. flour
Dash of red pepper
¾ c. sesame seed

Cream cheese with butter. Add flour, salt, and red pepper. Mix until well blended. Form into 1-inch balls, and roll in sesame seed. Chill for at least 2 hours. Bake on greased cookie sheet in a 400° oven for 10 to 12 minutes. Makes about 3 dozen.

KNISHES

3 c. flour
1 t. baking powder
½ t. salt
1 c. water
1 egg, slightly beaten
Vegetable oil
Filling of choice
1 egg yolk mixed with 1 T. flour

Combine flour, baking powder, and salt in a large bowl. Add water, egg, and 1 tablespoon oil. Stir with wooden spoon until dough forms. Turn out on a lightly floured surface and knead until smooth and elastic, about 5 minutes, using only enough additional flour to keep dough from sticking. Cover dough and let rest 30 minutes. Divide dough into fourths and roll out one-fourth of dough on lightly floured surface to a 12-inch square. Cut in half to make 2 6-inch wide strips. Brush lightly with oil. Spoon filling down center of strip. Bring 1 side of pastry over filling, then roll up to enclose filling completely, pinch ends together. Place on a lightly greased cookie sheet, seam side down. Score with a knife at 1-inch intervals; do not cut through. Brush with egg yolk wash. Bake in a 375° oven 30 minutes or until golden brown. Cut into 1-inch pieces. Serve warm. Makes about 8 dozen.

POTATO FILLING

2 medium-size potatoes, cooked and mashed
2 T. vegetable oil
¾ c. finely chopped onion
¾ t. salt
⅛ t. pepper
1 T. minced parsley

Sauté onion in oil until tender, not brown. Combine all ingredients, mixing well. Makes enough filling for 24 Knishes.

KASHA FILLING

1 c. cooked Kasha
¾ c. finely chopped onion
2 T. vegetable oil
¾ t. salt
¼ t. pepper

Sauté onion in oil until golden brown. Stir into Kasha with salt and pepper. Makes enough filling for 24 Knishes.

CHEESE FILLING

1 3-oz. pkg. cream cheese
½ c. small-curd cottage cheese
1 egg yolk
1 t. sugar
¼ t. salt
¼ t. vanilla

Beat all ingredients together until smooth. Makes enough filling for 24 Knishes.

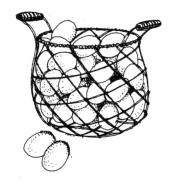

SPINACH PARMESAN APPETIZER PIE

4 green onions, snipped
4 T. butter or margarine
¼ lb. mushrooms, chopped
1 pkg. frozen spinach, thawed, drained
1 clove garlic, minced
¼ t. tarragon
3 T. minced parsley
4 eggs
½ c. milk
1 t. salt
¼ t. pepper
½ c. shredded Parmesan cheese

Sauté onions in butter for 3 minutes; add mushrooms and sauté 5 minutes. Stir in spinach, garlic, tarragon, and parsley. Simmer over medium heat, stirring constantly until liquid evaporates. Beat eggs with milk, salt, and pepper; add cheese. Combine with sautéed vegetables and pour into a lightly buttered 9-inch pie pan. Bake in a 375° oven for 35 to 40 minutes or until a knife inserted in center comes out clean. Cut in wedges and serve on individual plates with forks. Makes 6 to 9 servings.

*Pictured opposite:
Spinach Parmesan Appetizer Pie*

BACON ROLL UPS

10 slices white bread, crusts removed
½ lb. hot sausage, cooked and drained
1 8-oz. pkg. cream cheese, softened
10 slices bacon, cut in quarters

Cut bread slices into 4 fingers. Spread with mixture of sausage and cream cheese. Place each bread strip on top of a bacon strip; roll jelly-roll fashion. Secure with a toothpick. Bake in a 400° oven for 15 to 20 minutes until brown and crispy. Makes 40 Bacon Roll Ups.

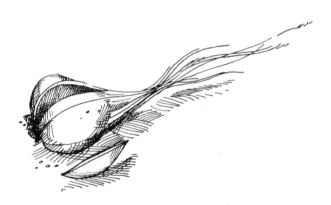

ASPARAGUS ROLLS

1 T. lemon juice
1 T. minced onion
   Salt to taste
½ c. butter or margarine, softened
25 slices white bread, crusts removed
1 15-oz. can white asparagus spears, drained
¼ c. melted butter

Stir lemon juice and onion into butter; season to taste with salt. Roll bread slice flat with rolling pin, spread 1 teaspoon of butter mixture on one side of bread. Place an asparagus spear on one end and roll up tightly. Brush rolls with melted butter and place on ungreased baking sheet. Bake rolls in a 350° oven for 30 minutes, turning every 10 minutes to brown evenly. May be frozen after baking and reheated for 20 minutes at 350°. Makes 25 rolls.

DEVILED TOAST

½ c. butter, softened
1 t. Worcestershire sauce
½ c. sesame seed
1 loaf very thin-sliced bread, crusts removed

Mix together butter, Worcestershire sauce, and sesame seed. Spread on bread slices. Cut each slice into quarters or fingers. Bake in a 325° oven for 25 to 30 minutes until crisp and golden brown. Makes 5 to 6 dozen.

DEVILED BLUE CHEESE NIBBLES

1 8-oz. pkg. refrigerator biscuits, cut into quarters
¼ c. butter
¼ c. blue cheese
1 t. Worcestershire sauce

Arrange biscuits in a cake pan so they touch each other. Melt butter and cheese, add Worcestershire sauce. Pour cheese mixture over biscuits. Bake in a 400° oven for 12 to 15 minutes until golden. Serve hot. Makes 40.

EGG CUPS

4 green onions, sliced
¼ lb. mushrooms, minced
2 T. butter
2 slices smoked salmon, minced
6 eggs
4 T. cold water
   Freshly ground pepper
12 Toast Cups

Sauté onions and mushrooms in butter. Add salmon, and warm through. Beat eggs with cold water until light. Pour over onion mixture; add pepper to taste and scramble lightly. Spoon into toast cups. Makes 12.

TOAST CUPS

Trim 12 slices of white bread. Butter both sides. Fit slices into muffin tins, pressing sides and bottom gently. Toast in a 400° oven for 5 to 8 minutes or until golden brown.

Nuts

VIRGINIA PEANUTS

1 to 2 lbs. shelled peanuts
¼ c. butter
Salt

Soak peanuts in water to cover for 24 hours; drain. Place on a non-stick cookie sheet; dot with butter. Roast in a 325° oven, stirring occasionally for 30 to 40 minutes. Remove and sprinkle with salt. Makes 4 to 8 cups.

STUFFED PECANS

1 lb. large pecan halves
1 3 to 4-oz. pkg. sharp Cheddar cheese spread
2 T. minced onion
Few drops Worcestershire sauce

Mix cheese and seasoning until smooth. Place a dollop between 2 nut halves. Chill and serve. Makes about 4 cups.

SNAPPY MIX

¼ lb. margarine
2 t. Worcestershire sauce
¼ to ½ t. Tabasco sauce
2 cloves garlic, crushed
4 to 6 c. popped corn
1 8 to 12-oz. pkg. corn chips
2 c. miniature pretzels
1 3-oz. can chow mein noodles
1 c. toasted soybeans (optional)

In a saucepan, melt margarine; add sauces and garlic. Mix remaining ingredients in a large roasting pan and pour spicy mixture over all until well-coated. Bake in a 250° oven for 1 hour stirring several times. Cool and store in airtight containers. Makes about 8 cups.

SAUTÉED NUTS

2 c. almonds, walnuts or pecans
4 T. butter
1 t. salt
1 t. ginger, curry powder, or garlic powder

Combine nuts and butter. Place in shallow pan in a 350° oven and bake for 30 minutes or until golden brown. Stir occasionally. Drain on absorbent paper and sprinkle with salt and seasoning. Makes about 2 cups.

Seafood

CURRIED TUNA SANDWICHES

1 7-oz. can water packed tuna
½ c. mayonnaise
1 t. lemon juice
¼ t. curry powder
¼ t. prepared horseradish
¼ t. salt
12 slices white bread cut in circles
Softened butter or margarine

Drain and flake tuna. Combine all ingredients, except bread and butter. Spread each bread round with butter and tuna mixture. Tops may be decorated with sprig of parsley, bit of pimiento or olive slice. Makes 12 open-faced sandwiches.

TUNA-CHEESE BITES

1 6½-oz. can tuna
1 c. shredded Cheddar cheese
¼ c. butter, softened
2 T. lemon juice
1 T. minced onion
1 t. Worcestershire sauce
3 drops Tabasco sauce
30 toast rounds

Drain and flake tuna. Cream together cheese and butter. Add seasonings and tuna, mixing thoroughly. Spread each toast round with about 2 teaspoonfuls of the mixture. Place on a cookie sheet; broil about 4 inches from burner for 3 to 4 minutes or until lightly browned. Makes 30.

HERRING 'N SOUR CREAM

1 8 to 16-oz. jar herring in wine sauce
¼ c. mayonnaise
½ pt. sour cream
Juice of ½ lemon
½ green pepper, chopped
1 t. celery seed
1 t. sugar
4 green onions and tops, sliced

Rinse and drain herring. Combine all ingredients; marinate for up to 3 weeks in refrigerator. Serve with crackers. Makes 2 to 3 cups.

TUNA BALLS

2 13-oz. cans tuna
2 3-oz. pkgs. cream cheese, softened
1 T. lemon juice
2 T. horseradish
¼ t. Tabasco sauce
1 c. snipped parsley

Drain and flake tuna. Cream the cheese; add lemon juice, horseradish, Tabasco sauce, and tuna. Shape tuna-cheese mixture into small balls; roll in parsley. Chill several hours. Makes about 40.

Pictured opposite:
Herring 'N Sour Cream

TUNA PINWHEELS

6 slices thin sliced bread, crusts removed
  Butter or margarine
1 6-oz. can tuna or shrimp
¼ c. mayonnaise

Drain and mash tuna. Mix in mayonnaise. Butter bread and spread with tuna mixture. Roll bread up jelly-roll fashion. Wrap in plastic wrap; chill several hours or overnight. Slice to desired thickness and serve. Makes 2 dozen.

TUNA-DILL SPREAD

1 8-oz. pkg. cream cheese
1 13-oz. can tuna
1 T. dry sherry
1 T. lemon juice
½ t. garlic powder
½ t. dill weed
⅛ t. white pepper

Rinse and drain tuna. Combine all ingredients; beat until light and fluffy. Serve on toast or crackers. Makes about 2 cups.

CRAB STUFFED MUSHROOM

1 7½-oz. can crab meat
3 green onions, snipped
¼ c. grated Parmesan cheese
½ c. mayonnaise
12 jumbo mushroom caps, washed and dried
½ c. butter or margarine
  Parmesan cheese

Drain crab meat; remove cartilage. Mix crab meat, onion, and ¼ cup Parmesan cheese with mayonnaise. Lightly sauté mushroom caps in butter. Remove from pan and drain. Stuff caps with crab mixture. Place in an ungreased shallow pan. Bake in a 325° oven for 5 minutes. Sprinkle caps with Parmesan cheese and broil for 3 minutes. Makes 12.

CRAB MEAT PUFF

1 6-oz. can crab meat
1 3-oz. pkg. cream cheese, softened
¼ c. mayonnaise
1 t. minced onion
1 t. salt
⅛ t. pepper
1 T. snipped parsley
  Toast rounds

Combine all ingredients except toast rounds. Mound crab meat mixture on toast; broil until bubbly. Makes about 1 cup.

KING CRAB DIP

4 oz. whipped cream cheese with chives
¼ c. milk
1 10½-oz. can cream of celery soup
1 T. dry sherry
1 7½-oz. can Alaska king crab or
1 pkg. frozen king crab

Blend cream cheese, milk, and celery soup. Heat in saucepan, stirring until smooth; add sherry. Add crab and heat through. Serve warm in a chafing dish with toast or crackers. Makes 8 to 12 servings.

KING CRAB SANDWICH

1 7¾-oz. can king crab meat
1 T. mayonnaise
1 t. soy sauce
⅛ t. garlic powder
⅛ t. pepper
1 egg white, stiffly beaten
  Bread rounds, toasted on 1 side

Remove membrane from crab meat; set aside chunks of meat. Combine mayonnaise, soy sauce, garlic, and pepper. Fold in beaten egg white. Heap on untoasted side of bread round. Top with crab chunk; broil 2 minutes until puffy and golden. Serves 8.

CRAB STUFFED MUSHROOMS

24 large mushroom caps
   Juice of 1 lemon
½ lb. crab meat
½ c. mayonnaise
¼ c. minced celery
   Dash of Tabasco
½ c. minced parsley

Toss mushroom caps in lemon juice; set aside. Mix together crab meat, mayonnaise, celery, and Tabasco. Fill each cap with crab mixture. Chill and serve. Sprinkle with parsley just before serving. Makes 24.

CRAB DIP

½ lb. crab meat
1 T. snipped chives
½ c. mayonnaise
1 c. grated Cheddar cheese
¼ c. chili sauce
1 T. sherry

Mix together all ingredients. Heat over low heat until cheese melts. Serve with melba toast or French bread chunks. Serves 4 to 6.

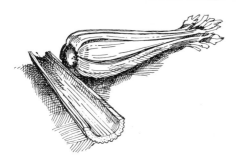

HOT CRAB DIP

1 6 to 8-oz. can crab meat, drained and flaked
2 T. lemon juice
1 c. sour cream
¼ c. mayonnaise
1 t. Worcestershire sauce
   Dash of Tabasco sauce
¼ c. snipped chives or parsley

Combine all ingredients except parsley or chives, mixing well. Heat to steaming; serve hot with melba toast or crackers. Serves 6 to 8.

CRAB MEAT DIP

1 8-oz. pkg. cream cheese, softened
⅛ t. salt
1 T. grated or minced onion
2 t. lemon juice
½ t. Worcestershire sauce
¾ c. sour cream or sour half and half
2 6½-oz. cans crab meat, minced

Combine all ingredients, mixing well; chill. Serve with crackers. Makes 2 cups.

HOT SHRIMP RAREBIT

1 10-oz. can tomato soup
1 c. grated Muenster cheese
½ lb. minced cooked shrimp
1 T. Worcestershire sauce

Melt soup and cheese together over low heat. Add shrimp and Worcestershire sauce. Serve hot with chunks of French bread. Serves 6 to 8.

PINK SHRIMP DIP

1 8-oz. pkg. cream cheese, softened
¼ c. mayonnaise
3 T. chili sauce
1 T. lemon juice
¼ t. Worcestershire sauce
   Dash of Tabasco sauce
1 can tiny shrimp, rinsed and drained

Combine all ingredients, blending well. Chill several hours. Serve with crackers or raw vegetables. Makes 1½ cups.

SHRIMP ROUNDS

24 cooked medium shrimp
½ to 1 c. Italian salad dressing
24 melba rounds, buttered
24 thin slices cucumber
   Dash of paprika

Marinate shrimp in salad dressing for 6 to 8 hours. Top melba toast with 1 slice cucumber and 1 shrimp. Sprinkle with paprika. Makes 24.

SHRIMP REMOULADE

1½ lbs. hot cooked shrimp
4 T. vegetable oil
2 T. olive oil
½ t. white pepper
½ t. salt
1 t. snipped parsley
½ t. horseradish
1 celery heart, minced
2 T. tarragon vinegar
4 T. brown mustard
½ c. snipped green onions

Combine all ingredients except shrimp; whip with a fork or whisk until well blended. Pour over hot shrimp. Shrimp should be hot so it will absorb the flavor of the marinade. Refrigerate in marinade. Serve chilled in individual seafood shells or on a serving dish. Makes 8 to 10 servings.

SEAFOOD COQUILLE

1 lb. scallops
3 T. snipped scallions
½ c. butter or margarine
1 lb. small cooked shrimp
3 T. flour
2 c. yogurt or sour cream
1 T. lemon juice
    Dash of Tabasco sauce
    Salt and pepper to taste
1 4-oz. can mushroom pieces, drained
12 patty shells
½ c. bread crumbs
½ c. grated Parmesan cheese

Put scallops in a saucepan and cover with water. Bring water to a boil and simmer scallops for 3 to 5 minutes or until they are firm. Drain. Sauté scallions in skillet with butter, adding the flour and blending well. Add shrimp, scallops and yogurt; blend well over low heat. Stir in seasonings and then the mushrooms. Spoon into individual shells; sprinkle with bread crumbs and cheese. Put shells on a cookie sheet; place under the broiler until the cheese browns. Makes 12 servings.

SHRIMP

5 c. water or 2 c. beer plus 3 c. water
2 T. horseradish
1 bay leaf
2 T. Worcestershire sauce
3 to 5 lbs. shrimp

In a large kettle, bring water to a rolling boil. Add horseradish, bay leaf, and Worcestershire sauce. Add shrimp and boil for 5 to 7 minutes. Drain immediately. Cool and shell shrimp. Chill shrimp; place on a bed of cracked ice. Spear with toothpicks to dip in sauce. Serves 15 to 20.

SHRIMP SAUCE

2 c. chili sauce
¼ c. horseradish
1 T. Worcestershire sauce
    Juice of ½ lemon
1 T. vinegar

Combine all ingredients and mix well.

SHRIMP PATÉ

3 c. cooked shrimp, minced
2 T. lemon juice
2 T. horseradish
¼ c. chili sauce
½ c. mayonnaise

Combine all ingredients. Chill and serve with cucumber or zucchini slices or crackers. Makes 4 cups paté.

SPANISH SAUCE FOR SHRIMP

1 c. mayonnaise
½ c. catsup
¼ c. chili sauce
½ c. chopped pimiento-stuffed olives
1 T. brandy
½ t. prepared mustard
½ t. Worcestershire sauce
½ t. lemon juice
    Dash of freshly ground pepper

Mix all ingredients together and chill. Makes about 1¾ cups.

HOT SHRIMP DIP

¼ c. butter
1 small onion, minced
½ lb. chopped cooked shrimp
½ c. grated processed Swiss cheese
¼ c. cocktail sauce

Sauté onion in butter. Add shrimp, cheese, and cocktail sauce. Cook over low heat until cheese melts. Serve hot with crackers. Serves 4 to 6.

SHRIMP BUTTER

¼ lb. butter or margarine, softened
1 4½-oz. can shrimp
¼ t. dill weed
2 t. lemon juice
Freshly ground pepper to taste

Wash and drain shrimp; chop. Blend all ingredients together and chill. Bring to room temperature 30 minutes before serving. Serve on crackers or bread. Makes about 1 cup.

SHRIMP DE JONGHE

2 lbs. shrimp, cooked and cleaned
¼ c. butter
¾ c. cold butter
1 clove garlic, minced
¾ c. dry sherry
½ c. minced parsley
1½ c. lightly toasted bread crumbs
¼ c. grated Parmesan cheese
¼ c. melted butter

Sauté shrimp lightly in ¼ cup butter. Place in 8 individual ramekins or shells. Beat cold butter until light and gradually add the garlic, sherry, parsley, and bread crumbs. Spoon bread mixture over the shrimp, spreading with a knife. Sprinkle with grated Parmesan and drizzle with melted butter. Bake in a 350° oven for about 30 minutes. May be prepared early in the day, refrigerated, brought to room temperature, and then baked. Serves 8.

SHRIMP-CHEESE CANAPES

30 bread rounds
1 c. chopped cooked shrimp
½ c. grated American or Cheddar cheese
1 T. minced celery
1 T. minced onion
3 T. mayonnaise
¼ t. dry mustard
¼ t. lemon juice
¼ t. Worcestershire sauce

Toast bread rounds on one side. Mix remaining ingredients together; spread on untoasted side of bread. Place 4 inches beneath broiler; broil for about 4 minutes. Makes 30 canapes.

ANCHOVY MELBA

¼ c. butter or margarine, softened
1 T. anchovy paste
24 slices of melba toast

Combine butter and anchovy paste, mixing well. Spread thinly on melba toast. Makes 24 appetizers.

DEVILED SHRIMP

2 lbs. shrimp, cooked and still warm
1 lemon, thinly sliced
1 red onion, thinly sliced
½ c. fresh lemon juice
¼ c. vegetable oil (olive oil may be used)
1 T. wine vinegar
1 garlic clove, minced
½ bay leaf
1 T. dry mustard
¼ t. cayenne
1 t. salt
Freshly ground pepper

Put shrimp, lemon and onion slices in a serving bowl. Combine lemon juice, oil, vinegar, spices, and herbs, and mix together well. Pour over the shrimp mixture. Cover and chill at least 2 hours, stirring once or twice.

PUFFY SHRIMP

1 can crescent roll dough
1 4½-oz. can shrimp
1 egg white
⅓ c. mayonnaise
1 T. finely chopped celery
2 t. snipped green onions or chives
½ t. mustard
½ t. cream-style horseradish

Wash and drain shrimp. Separate dough into 8 triangles. Cut each in half to form 16 triangles. Place on an ungreased cookie sheet. Beat egg white until soft peaks form. Fold mayonnaise, celery, onion, mustard, and horseradish into egg white. Spread mixture on triangles; top with 2 shrimp. Bake in a 375° oven for 15 to 18 minutes. Serve warm. Makes 16.

SARDINE DIP

1 c. creamed cottage cheese
1 3¾-oz. can sardines, undrained, mashed
1 T. lemon juice
1 T. minced onion
Dash of Tabasco sauce
¼ t. pepper

Combine all ingredients, mixing well. Chill and serve with crackers or rye bread. Serves 6 to 8.

SARDINE PASTE

1 8-oz. pkg. cream cheese, softened
½ t. salt
2 T. lemon juice
1 t. garlic powder
2 3¾-oz. cans sardines (boneless and skinless), mashed
⅛ t. Tabasco sauce

Combine all ingredients, mixing well. Spread on toast rounds. Makes about 2 cups.

CAVIAR BALL

¼ t. bouillon crystals
1 t. hot water
1 8-oz. pkg. cream cheese
¼ t. minced onion
1 T. mayonnaise
2 4-oz. jars red or black caviar

Dissolve bouillon in hot water. Cream together cream cheese, bouillon, onion, and mayonnaise; shape into a ball. Frost completely with the caviar. Place on a bed of endive or romaine. Serve with rye saltines or melba toast. Serves 8 to 12.

HALIBUT VINAIGRETTE

Prepare this appetizer at least 2 days before serving.

2 lbs. halibut steak, ½ inch thick
1 t. salt
¼ c. salad oil
1 large Spanish onion, thinly sliced
2 T. olive oil
2 cloves garlic, minced
¾ c. white wine vinegar
1 t. paprika
1 t. salt
½ t. freshly ground pepper

Sprinkle halibut steak on both sides with 1 teaspoon salt; let stand 15 minutes. In a large skillet, heat salad oil and sauté halibut 5 minutes on each side. Place on a dish and refrigerate. Sauté onion in olive oil until tender. Stir in garlic, vinegar, paprika, salt, and pepper; cool. Remove skin and bone from halibut and break into chunks. Arrange fish and onion mixtures in layers in a glass bowl. Refrigerate, covered, for at least 2 days. It keeps in refrigerator for 2 weeks. Serves 8.

CHILI CLAM DIP

1 8-oz. pkg. cream cheese, softened
1 8-oz. can minced clams and juice
1 bottle chili sauce
1 T. lemon juice

Mix together all ingredients well. Serve with corn chips or crackers. Serves 4 to 6.

CLAM FONDUE

2 T. butter
1 T. vegetable oil
¼ c. minced onion
½ green pepper, diced
½ lb. Cheddar cheese, shredded
4 T. catsup
1 T. Worcestershire sauce
Dash of Tabasco sauce
2 8-oz. cans chopped clams, drained
2 T. dry sherry
1 loaf French or Italian bread, cubed

In top of double boiler, chafing dish, or fondue pot, heat butter and oil. Sauté onion and green pepper until soft. Add a small amount of cheese at a time with catsup, Worcestershire sauce, and Tabasco sauce. Stir constantly until cheese melts. Just before serving, add clams and sherry. Dip cubes of bread in fondue. Serves 8 to 10.

ARTICHOKE-CLAM PUFFS

2 10-oz. pkgs. frozen artichoke hearts
1 8-oz. pkg. cream cheese, softened
¼ t. Tabasco sauce
2 T. sherry
1 6½-oz. can drained minced clams
3 T. grated Parmesan cheese, or paprika

Cook artichokes according to package directions until just barely tender. Drain and place on broil-and-serve platter. Beat cheese with Tabasco and sherry; stir in clams. Spoon mixture onto cut sides of artichokes. Sprinkle with Parmesan or paprika; broil until browned. Makes about 36.

ROASTED OYSTERS

Oysters
Melted butter

Place oysters on a cookie sheet in 350° oven for a few minutes until they pop open. Finish opening and serve with melted butter for dipping.

SCALLOPED OYSTERS

1½ c. coarse cracker crumbs
½ c. grated Parmesan cheese
¼ c. melted butter or margarine
½ t. salt
Dash of pepper
1 pt. drained fresh oysters
¼ c. dry sherry
½ c. yogurt or sour cream
1 T. butter or margarine
8 patty shells

Combine crumbs, cheese, ¼ c. butter, salt, and pepper in a skillet. Stir until well mixed. Spread half of the crumb mixture on the bottoms of 8 shells. Spoon oysters over crumbs. Combine the sherry and yogurt and spoon on top of the oysters. Top with remaining crumbs. Dot with bits of butter. Place shells on a cookie sheet and bake in a 375° oven for 20 minutes until crumbs are golden brown. Serves 8.

OYSTERS ON THE HALF SHELL

Oysters
Lemon wedges

Open fresh oysters, and place on a large tray of cracked ice. Serve with cocktail picks and lemon wedges, and bowls of horseradish, catsup, and vinegar.

Pictured opposite:
Oysters on the Half Shell

SALAD NICOISE

Salad greens to line a platter
2 6½-oz. cans tuna fish, drained
1 can sardines, drained, optional
12 pitted ripe olives
3 hard-boiled eggs, quartered
1 green pepper, cut in strips
12 cherry tomatoes
1 red onion, sliced in thin rings
8 to 10 anchovy fillets, drained
1 jar marinated artichoke hearts,
  reserve juice
2 to 4 T. wine vinegar

Arrange tuna, sardines, olives, eggs, green pepper, cherry tomatoes, onion, anchovy fillets, and artichoke hearts attractively on the salad greens. Combine artichoke juice and vinegar; pour over vegetables. Serves 8 to 12.

CRAB MEAT HORS D'OEUVRES

15 slices white bread, crusts removed
6 oz. crab meat, flaked
1 small onion, grated
1 c. grated Cheddar cheese
1 c. mayonnaise
1 t. curry powder
½ t. salt

Cut bread into 4 squares. Combine remaining ingredients and spread on bread. Broil until golden and bubbly. Makes 60 hors d'oeuvres.

OYSTER CANAPÉS

Squares of thinly sliced dark
  bread, buttered
Red or black caviar
1 can smoked oysters

Border each bread square with caviar. In the center, place 1 oyster. Cover oyster with a dollop of sour cream or mayonnaise.

ANCHOVY CANAPÉS

1 small tin anchovy fillets, drained
1 3-oz. pkg. cream cheese, softened
1 green onion, snipped
1 T. sour cream
  Pinch of curry powder
  Buttered bread rounds
1 t. minced parsley
  Paprika

Mash anchovies. Add to cream cheese together with onion, sour cream, and curry powder. Beat until smooth. Spread on rounds of buttered bread. Sprinkle with parsley and lightly with paprika. Chill. Serves about 6.

SMOKED FISH CANAPÉS

Smoked whitefish, carp, trout or other
  smoked fish
Butter, softened
Paprika
Parsley, minced

Mash fish in proportion of 1 teaspoon fish to 2 tablespoons butter. Spread on bread rounds and sprinkle with paprika and minced parsley.

NOVA SCOTIA SALMON AND ONION CHEESECAKE

Butter
½ c. fine bread crumbs
3½ 8-oz. pkgs. cream cheese, softened (28 oz.)
4 large eggs
⅓ c. heavy cream
½ c. chopped onion
½ green pepper, chopped
2 T. butter
¼ lb. Nova Scotia salmon, diced
½ c. grated Gruyere cheese
3 T. grated Parmesan cheese
Salt and pepper

Butter the inside of an 8 x 8 x 3-inch cheesecake pan. Sprinkle the bottom and sides with crumbs. Mix cream cheese, eggs, and cream with electric mixer until smooth. Set aside. Sauté onion and green pepper in 2 tablespoons butter. Fold the salmon, Gruyere cheese, Parmesan cheese, sautéed onion, and green pepper into the cheese cake mixture. Add salt and pepper to taste. Pour batter into prepared pan; tap gently to level mixture. Set pan into a larger pan (so edges do not touch); add 2 inches of boiling water to larger pan. Bake in a 300° oven for 1 hour and 40 minutes. Turn off oven and let cake remain in oven for 1 hour longer. Lift cake out of water; place on rack to cool at least 2 hours before unmolding. Makes 12 to 20 servings.

BACON BLUE CHEESE CHEESECAKE

½ lb. bacon, cooked and chopped
½ c. finely chopped onion
½ lb. blue cheese, crumbled
Salt and freshly ground pepper to taste
2 to 3 drops Tabasco sauce

Sauté onion in 1 tablespoon bacon fat until soft. To the basic cheese mixture, add bacon, onion, blue cheese, salt, pepper, and Tabasco sauce, blending thoroughly. Pour into pan and bake as directed above.

CRUNCHY SALMON SPREAD

16 rounds of bread or toast, buttered
1 1-lb. can salmon, drained and flaked
1 8-oz. can water chestnuts, drained and chopped
1 small onion, minced
1 stalk celery, minced
½ c. mayonnaise
2 T. soy sauce
1 T. lemon juice

Combine all ingredients, except bread. Spread salmon mixture on bread or toast rounds. Sprinkle snipped parsley on top. Makes 16 rounds.

SALMON NEWBURG

8 T. butter
6 T. flour
4 c. cream
5 T. grated Parmesan cheese
1 T. paprika
1 t. dry mustard
Salt to taste
Dash of Tabasco sauce
6 egg yolks, beaten
4 T. brandy
4 T. dry sherry
6 c. salmon, drained and flaked

Melt butter in a saucepan and stir in flour. Cook for 7 minutes without letting flour brown. Gradually add warm cream, stirring constantly until sauce is thick and smooth. Add Parmesan, paprika, mustard, salt, and Tabasco. Pour the sauce slowly over beaten egg yolks, stirring constantly. Add brandy and sherry. Stir in salmon; heat thoroughly. Place in chafing dish. Serve with toast rounds or patty shells. Serves 24.

SCANDINAVIAN SALMON

1 T. salt
1 T. sugar
1½ t. whole peppercorns, crushed
1 T. dill weed
1 lb. raw salmon fillets

Mix together salt, sugar, pepper, and dill. Place fish on a large piece of heavy foil. Cover with seasonings. Close foil; place on tray or in a shallow dish. Weight down with 3 to 4 unopened heavy cans. Refrigerate 48 hours. Scrape off seasonings, slice thin and serve with toast and lemon wedges. Serves 10 to 12.

SALMON SPREAD

1 1-lb. can salmon, drained and flaked
1 unpeeled cucumber, grated
1 3-oz. pkg. cream cheese
½ c. mayonnaise
1 T. dry white wine
¼ t. pepper
¼ t. tarragon
¼ c. minced parsley
¼ c. snipped chives

Remove skin and bones from salmon. Mix together all ingredients except parsley and chives. Spoon into serving bowl, sprinkle with parsley and chives. Serve cold with crackers. Serves 12 to 16.

DILLY SALMON SPREAD

1 15½-oz. can salmon
1 c. sour cream or sour half and half
½ c. chopped celery
2 T. lemon juice
1 t. Worcestershire sauce
½ t. dill weed
¼ t. salt

Drain and flake salmon. Add sour cream, celery, and seasonings. Mix thoroughly and chill. Serve with chips, crackers or vegetables. Makes 2½ cups.

CURRIED SALMON SPREAD

1 1-lb. can salmon, drained and flaked
1 stalk celery, minced
2 green onions, snipped
¼ c. mayonnaise
¼ c. sour cream
1 T. lemon juice
1 t. curry powder
Dash of pepper

Remove skin and bones from salmon. Mix together all ingredients well. Serve with toast rounds or crackers. Serves 12 to 16.

NOVA PINWHEELS

1 lb. smoked salmon
1 8-oz. pkg. cream cheese, softened
2 T. sour cream, mayonnaise, or yogurt

Blend together cheese and sour cream. Spread mixture on individual strips of salmon; roll up jelly-roll fashion. Cut in ½ inch slices. Place pinwheel flat on buttered party rye slices.

SALMON MOUSSE

2 T. gelatin
¼ c. cold water
1 15½-oz. can salmon
1 10¾-oz. can tomato soup
1 8-oz. pkg. cream cheese, softened
1 c. mayonnaise
1 green pepper, finely chopped
1 c. chopped celery
1 small onion, grated
1 T. Worcestershire sauce
½ t. salt
¼ t. white pepper

Dissolve gelatin in water. Drain and flake salmon. Heat soup and cream cheese over low heat until cheese is dissolved. Add softened gelatin and stir until well blended. Add remaining ingredients and mix well. Place in a well-greased fish mold; chill overnight in the refrigerator. Unmold on bed of endive or leaf lettuce. Serve with toast. Serves 12 to 16.

Pictured opposite:
Salmon Mousse

Vegetables

PEPPER CRESCENTS

6 medium green peppers
1 4-oz. pkg. blue cheese, softened
1 8-oz. pkg. cream cheese, softened
1 8-oz. pkg. Cheddar cheese spread, softened
2 T. mayonnaise
1 t. mustard

Wash green peppers, cut each in half lengthwise and remove seeds. Blend cheeses, mayonnaise, and mustard together. Spoon into pepper shells. Chill until firm; slice each shell lengthwise into crescents. Makes 24 crescents.

RATATOUILLE

4 T. olive oil
1 large onion, chopped
1 clove garlic, minced
1 green pepper, chopped
1 medium eggplant, chopped
3 ripe tomatoes, chopped
2 zucchini, chopped
½ t. basil
½ t. thyme
1 t. salt
1 T. lemon juice

Heat olive oil, add vegetables and seasonings, except lemon juice. Simmer slowly until thickened, 20 to 40 minutes. Sprinkle with lemon juice, chill. Serve with crackers. Makes 24 to 36 servings.

CORSICAN COMBO

2 6¾-oz. cans pitted ripe olives, drained
1 pt. cherry tomatoes
¼ c. minced fresh parsley

Wash and stem tomatoes. Marinate olives and tomatoes in marinade for 12 to 24 hours. Just before serving, garnish with parsley. Serves 8 to 10.

MARINADE

½ c. wine vinegar
1 c. olive oil
1 clove garlic, cut
1 bay leaf
1 t. basil

Combine all ingredients, mixing well.

STUFFED CELERY

1 stalk celery
1 4-oz. pkg. blue cheese, crumbled
1 c. yogurt or sour cream
¼ c. finely snipped green onions or chives
1 T. brandy

Combine all ingredients except celery, and chill until of spreading consistency. Cut celery into 2-inch pieces, fill with blue cheese/yogurt mixture, and serve cold. Makes 6 to 7 dozen.
Note: For variation, stuff celery with sharp cheese spread and sprinkle with chopped nuts.

CARROT STIX PROVENCALE

1 lb. carrots, cut into sticks
1¼ c. sauterne
¼ c. water
1 clove garlic, minced
1 t. seasoning salt
1 t. sugar
2 T. olive oil
⅛ t. dry mustard
1 bay leaf
2 T. snipped parsley

Bring all ingredients except carrots and parsley, to a boil; simmer for 5 minutes. Add carrots and simmer for 6 minutes longer. Cool, refrigerate, stirring in snipped parsley.

MIDDLE EAST SPREAD

1 1-lb. eggplant, unpeeled and diced
1 onion, chopped
2 to 3 T. vegetable oil
1 green pepper, chopped
1 red pepper, chopped
1 clove garlic, minced
1 t. salt
Pepper to taste
½ of a 15-oz. can tomato sauce with tomato bits

Salt and drain eggplant. Sauté onion in oil until golden brown. Add eggplant and sauté. Add peppers, garlic, salt, pepper, and tomato sauce. Cover and simmer until tender, about 10 minutes. Stir and chill for about 1 hour before serving. Add more salt if desired. Serves 4 to 6.

COCKTAIL BEETS

2 1-lb. cans small whole beets, drained
1 8-oz. pkg. cream cheese, softened
2 T. horseradish
1 T. mayonnaise

Combine cream cheese, horseradish and mayonnaise, mixing well. Scoop center out of beets and fill with cream cheese mixture. Serves 4 to 6.

PICKLED CARROT STIX

1 lb. carrots
¾ c. vinegar
¾ c. water
½ c. sugar
1 t. mixed whole pickling spice

Peel carrots; cut into sticks. Combine remaining ingredients and bring to a boil; simmer for 5 minutes. Place carrots in a dish, cover with hot liquid. Cool and refrigerate for a few days before serving. Serves 10.

COCKTAIL TOMATOES

12 cherry tomatoes
24 tiny cooked shrimp
¼ c. plain yogurt
1 T. minced onion
½ t. dried dill weed
⅛ t. salt

Scoop out centers of cherry tomatoes; invert and drain. Drain and wash shrimp. Combine yogurt, onion, dill, and salt. Fill tomato with the yogurt mixture, top with 2 shrimp each. Makes 12 Cocktail Tomatoes.

ARTICHOKE PRETTIES

1 10-oz. pkg. frozen artichoke hearts, cooked, drained, chilled
½ c. sour cream
½ c. red or black caviar
½ t. lemon juice
1 T. minced onion

Mix sour cream, caviar, lemon juice, and onion together. Spoon a little mixture into the cavity of each artichoke heart. Makes 4 to 6 servings.

TOMATO ROUNDS

36 rounds of thin white bread, buttered
36 slices of ripe tomato
½ c. mayonnaise
2 T. minced fresh basil

Top bread with tomatoes; garnish with mayonnaise spiced with fresh basil. Makes 36 rounds.

CUCUMBER SANDWICHES I

1 large cucumber, peeled
1 8-oz. pkg. cream cheese, softened
½ t. garlic salt
½ t. Worcestershire sauce
1 t. salt
¼ c. snipped green onion stems or snipped chives
30 rounds or fingers of white bread, buttered

Cut cucumber in half lengthwise; remove seeds. Dice and drain in a strainer for at least 1 hour. Mix cream cheese, garlic salt, Worcestershire sauce, and salt until well blended. Stir in drained cucumber and snipped onion. Spread on buttered bread rounds. Make open faced or closed sandwiches. Refrigerate covered with waxed paper and a damp cloth, until serving time. Makes about 2½ dozen.

CUCUMBER SANDWICHES II

48 thin rounds of pumpernickel, buttered
1 large cucumber
Minced chives

Score cucumber and slice thin. Marinate cucumber slices in marinade for at least 3 hours. Drain and place one slice of cucumber on each bread round. Top with a sprinkle of minced chives. Makes 48 sandwiches.

MARINADE

1 medium onion, minced
1 c. vinegar
Salt and pepper to taste

Combine all ingredients and mix well.

ONION SANDWICHES

48 slices of party pumpernickel, buttered
1 sweet red onion, minced
1 c. mayonnaise
1 c. minced parsley

Combine onion and mayonnaise. Spread on bread; garnish with parsley. Chill. Makes 48 sandwiches.

CUCUMBER RING

1 envelope unflavored gelatin
½ c. cold water
½ t. salt
4 c. creamed cottage cheese
2 3-oz. pkgs. cream cheese, softened
½ c. mayonnaise
1 medium cucumber
1 green onion, snipped
⅔ c. finely chopped celery

Soften gelatin in water. Add salt. Heat and stir over low heat until gelatin is dissolved. Beat cheeses together; add mayonnaise and gelatin. Pare and seed cucumber and grate. Stir in cucumber, onion, and celery. Pour into a lightly oiled 6-cup ring mold. Chill 6 to 8 hours or overnight. Garnish with cherry tomatoes and radishes. Serve with crackers. Serves 12.

STUFFED CUCUMBER

1 cucumber
1 3-oz. pkg. cream cheese, softened
1 T. mayonnaise
1 T. snipped green onion or chives
Snipped parsley

Combine cream cheese, mayonnaise, and green onion. Score cucumber with fork lengthwise. Cut in half and remove seeds with spoon. Fill cavity with cheese mixture, packing tightly. Chill several hours. Slice ¼-inch thick and sprinkle tops with snipped parsley. Makes 6 to 10 servings.

Pictured opposite:
Tomato Rounds
Cucumber Sandwiches I
Cucumber Sandwiches II

ENA'S IKRA

3 to 4 medium zucchini
2 to 3 T. vegetable oil
1 medium onion
1 tomato
1 t. vinegar
Salt and pepper to taste

Peel and slice zucchini. Sauté zucchini in oil until golden brown. Process zucchini, tomato and onion in food processor or put through meat grinder. Add vinegar, salt, and pepper. Serve with toast. Makes 10 to 12 servings.

MUSHROOM TIDBITS

1 8-oz. pkg. cream cheese, softened
1 T. snipped green onions or chives
1 T. butter or margarine, softened
1 3-oz. can chopped mushrooms, drained
¼ t. garlic powder

Combine all ingredients, mixing well. Spread on crackers. Sprinkle with paprika. Broil 3 to 5 minutes. Makes about 36.

MUSHROOMS FLORENTINE

2 pkgs. frozen chopped spinach
1 t. instant chicken bouillon
36 large mushrooms
4 T. butter or margarine
¼ t. garlic powder
¼ t. dry mustard
¼ t. seasoned salt
Parmesan cheese, grated

Clean mushrooms, separate stems and caps. Cook spinach as directed on package, adding chicken bouillon to the water. Drain well. Chop mushroom stems and sauté in butter. Combine spinach and seasonings. Lightly sauté mushroom caps in butter or margarine until slightly browned; drain. Fill caps with spinach mixture and sprinkle with Parmesan cheese. Place in a shallow pan and bake in a 375° oven for 15 minutes. Makes 36 appetizers.

WATER CHESTNUTS AND BACON

1 8-oz. can water chestnuts, drained
½ lb. bacon
½ c. soy sauce

Cut slices of bacon just long enough to encircle and overlap water chestnuts. Secure the bacon with a toothpick. Place in a bowl of soy sauce for several hours. Remove from sauce and broil until crisp. Makes 32 servings.

MARINATED MUSHROOMS I

1 lb. small mushrooms, cleaned and dried
½ c. olive oil
2 T. lemon juice
2 T. vinegar
1 t. salt
½ t. freshly ground pepper
¼ t. thyme
1 t. tarragon

Combine all ingredients and simmer over low heat for 5 to 10 minutes. Cool; refrigerate in marinade overnight. Bring to room temperature before serving. Makes 32 to 38 mushrooms.

MUSHROOM CAPERS

18 to 24 large mushrooms, washed and dried
⅓ c. fine dry bread crumbs
1 T. lemon juice
⅛ t. garlic powder
⅛ t. rosemary
⅛ t. marjoram
¼ t. salt
¼ c. almonds, finely chopped
1 T. capers, minced
Butter
Parsley

Chop mushroom stems and combine with remaining ingredients. Spoon mixture into mushroom caps. Place in a greased shallow baking pan. Dot each mushroom with butter and bake in a 350° oven for 20 minutes. To serve, sprinkle with snipped parsley. Makes 18 to 24.

MUSHROOM CAPS

12 large mushroom caps, washed and dried
1 3-oz. pkg. cream cheese, softened
½ t. curry powder or garlic powder
12 parsley sprigs

Combine cream cheese and curry powder. Fill mushroom caps with seasoned cream cheese. Garnish with a small sprig of parsley. Serves 6.

MUSHROOM CAVIAR

½ lb. mushrooms, minced
4 T. butter
2 T. minced onion
2 T. lemon juice
1 T. Worcestershire sauce
3 T. mayonnaise
½ t. salt
Dash of pepper

Sauté mushrooms in butter for about 5 minutes. Add onion, sauté for 5 more minutes. Remove from heat, cool slightly, drain. Add remaining ingredients. Mix well. Chill and serve with toast. Makes 1 to 1½ cups.

MARINATED MUSHROOMS II

1 lb. mushrooms, washed and dried
Snipped parsley

Pour vinaigrette dressing over mushrooms and allow to marinate for several hours. Pour off dressing. Sprinkle mushrooms with snipped parsley and serve on platter with toothpicks. Makes 32 to 38 mushrooms.

VINAIGRETTE DRESSING

2 T. red wine vinegar
6 T. olive oil
2 t. prepared mustard
2 t. lemon juice
1 t. salt
¼ t. freshly ground pepper

Combine all ingredients, mixing well.

MUSHROOM PATÉ

½ lb. mushrooms, sliced
2 T. margarine
1 8-oz. pkg. cream cheese, softened
1 t. minced onion
1 t. Worcestershire sauce
¼ t. garlic powder
2 slices white bread, cubed

Sauté mushrooms in margarine until tender. In blender or food processor, blend all ingredients until well mixed. Spoon into small bowl; cover and refrigerate until chilled. Serve with toast rounds. Makes 1½ cups.

HOT MUSHROOM CAPS

1 lb. mushrooms
2 T. butter or margarine
Garlic powder and pepper to taste

Clean and dry mushrooms. Separate caps and stems. Chop mushroom stems fine; sauté quickly in butter. Fill caps with seasoned sautéed stems and place in buttered baking dish. Heat in a 425° oven for 8 minutes. Serves 4 to 6.

VEGETABLES VINAIGRETTE

1 cucumber
3 carrots
½ head cauliflower
½ lb. string beans
1 lb. mushrooms, sliced
6 T. tarragon vinegar
½ c. vegetable oil
4 T. olive oil
4 T. lemon juice
1 t. sugar
1 T. salt
1 T. dill weed (optional)

Score cucumber and slice ¼ inch thick. Slice carrots in sticks or circles. Separate cauliflower and clean string beans. Combine vinegar, oils, lemon juice, sugar, salt, and dill weed; mix until blended. Pour over vegetables; marinate in refrigerator for up to three days. Serves 10 to 12.

Index

Pictured opposite:
Vegetables Vinaigrette, p. 61

VEGETABLES